ALGEBRA 1

Getting Ready for High-Stakes Assessment

Printed in the U.S.A.

ISBN   978-1-328-93851-0
2 3 4 5 6 7 8 9 10   0928   26 25 24 23 22 21 20 19
4500753934   A B C D E F G

Contents

Understand the relationship between zeros and factors of polynomials.

Create equations that describe numbers or relationships.

Understand solving equations as a process of reasoning and explain the reasoning.

Solve equations and inequalities in one variable.

Solve systems of equations.

Represent and solve equations and inequalities graphically.

Functions and Modeling

Understand the concept of a function and use function notation.

Interpret functions that arise in applications in terms of a context.

Analyze functions using different representations.

Build a function that models a relationship between two quantities.

Build new functions from existing functions.

Construct and compare linear, quadratic, and exponential models and solve problems.

Interpret expressions for functions in terms of the situation they model.

Statistics and Modeling

Summarize, represent, and interpret data on a single count or measurement variable.

Summarize, represent, and interpret data on two categorical and quantitative variables.

Interpret linear models.

Some of the items in the practice tests listed in the Contents also involve one or more of the following math processes and practices.

Math Processes and Practices

MPP1   Problem Solving

MPP2   Abstract and Quantitative Reasoning

MPP3   Using and Evaluating Logical Reasoning

MPP4   Mathematical Modeling

MPP5   Using Mathematical Tools

MPP6   Using Precise Mathematical Language

MPP7   Seeing Structure

MPP8   Generalizing

Preparing for High-Stakes Assessments

Your school district or state department of education may require you to take a test that is used to make important decisions, such as which students are eligible for a high school diploma or which teachers are rated as effective. Such tests are commonly called high-stakes assessments.

This *Getting Ready for High-Stakes Assessment* book provides opportunities to prepare for such tests based on what you learn in the math course you're taking. The following tables describe the types of assessment items in this book. Because you may be required to take a test online, the tables also explain how your online experience may differ from the way you complete the practice items in this book.

Each practice test consists of two broad categories of items: selected response and constructed response. Selected response items require you to make one or more choices from a group of options. Constructed response items require you to produce an answer on your own.

Type of Item in *Getting Ready for High-Stakes Assessment*	What Your Online Experience May Be Like

Multiple Choice (a type of selected response): You select the only correct answer from a list of answer choices.
 	
Example:
 	
Select the correct answer.
 	
1. What does the imaginary number *i* represent?
   Ⓐ -1
   Ⓑ $\sqrt{1}$
   Ⓒ $\sqrt{-1}$
   Ⓓ $-\sqrt{-1}$
	On a practice test in this book, you would fill in the oval containing the letter of the answer choice you select. For an online test, you would likely be presented with small circles (sometimes called "radio buttons"). Clicking on one of the circles causes the circle to be filled in.

Type of Item in *Getting Ready for High-Stakes Assessment*	What Your Online Experience May Be Like
Inline Multiple Choice (a type of selected response): This is a variation of Multiple Choice. Here, you make your selection from a list that appears within a sentence. Examples:	On a practice test in this book, you would circle the answer choice that makes a true statement. For an online test, you would likely be presented with a drop-down menu labeled "Choose..." or "Select One." Clicking on the menu displays a list of answer choices. You would then click on the answer choice you want to select.

1. Circle the ordered pair that makes a true statement.

   $\triangle ABC$ is shown below. Suppose the triangle is translated 5 units to the right and 7 units down. The coordinates of the image of vertex C after this

   transformation are
   $$\begin{array}{c}(-8,-6)\\(2,-6)\\(-3,-6)\\(2,0)\end{array}$$.

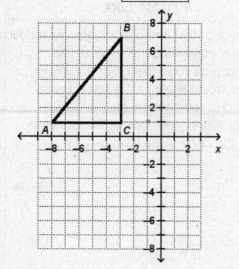

Type of Item in *Getting Ready for High-Stakes Assessment*	What Your Online Experience May Be Like
Multiple Response (a type of selected response): You select all correct answers from a list of possible answers. Examples:	On a practice test in this book, you would make selections by filling in ovals or circling answer choices. For an online test, you might be presented with "hot spots." The "hot spots" are boxes containing answer choices that light up when you click on them. Alternatively, each answer choice might have a small square next to it. Clicking the squares causes check marks to appear in them to indicate that you have selected those answer choices.

Select all correct answers.

3. Consider the directed line segment from $M(-3, 1)$ to $N(3, 4)$. Determine which of the following statements are true.

Ⓐ The point $P(1, 3)$ partitions the segment in the ratio 2 to 1.

Ⓑ The point $Q(-1, 2)$ partitions the segment in the ratio 1 to 2.

Ⓒ The point $R(0, 2.5)$ partitions the segment in the ratio 1 to 2.

Ⓓ The point $S(0, 2.5)$ partitions the segment in the ratio 1 to 1.

Ⓔ The point $T(-1, 4.5)$ partitions the segment in the ratio 1 to 1.

4. Circle each expression that is equal to $\left(p^{-3}\right)^{\frac{2}{5}}$. Assume that p is positive.

$$\sqrt[5]{p^{-6}} \qquad \sqrt[5]{p^{-13}}$$

$$\frac{1}{\sqrt{p^{15}}} \qquad \frac{1}{p\sqrt[5]{p}}$$

$$\frac{1}{p^{30}} \qquad \sqrt[10]{p^{-1}}$$

Type of Item in *Getting Ready for High-Stakes Assessment*	What Your Online Experience May Be Like
Categorization (a type of selected response): You assign given objects to categories by making a series of Yes/No, True/False, or Category A/Category B choices. Sometimes there may be more than two categories, such as True/False/Cannot Be Determined. Examples: 4. Consider the function $f(x) = 2x^2 + 4x - 30$. Indicate whether each statement is true of false by putting a check mark in the appropriate column of the table. 		True	False
---	---	---
The vertex of the graph is (1, –32).		
The zeros are 3 and –5.		
The graph opens down.		
The axis of symmetry is $x = -1$.		
The y-intercept is –30.		| 5. Indicate whether each of the following is rational or irrational by putting a check mark in the appropriate column of the table. |	Rational	Irrational
---	---	---
The product of $\sqrt{2}$ and 5		
$f(x) = x^2 + 2$ evaluated at $x = \sqrt{7}$		
The sum of $\sqrt{10}$ and $\sqrt{16}$		
$f(r) = \pi r^2$ evaluated at $r = 3$				On a practice test in this book, you would put a check mark in the appropriate column for the given object in each row of a table. For an online test, each cell of the table might have a small square that displays a check mark when you click on it. Alternatively, each cell might have a small circle that fills in when you click on it.

Type of Item in *Getting Ready for High-Stakes Assessment*	What Your Online Experience May Be Like

Matching (a type of selected response): You match an answer choice with each given object.

Examples:

Match each equation with the description of the circle it represents.

____ 4. $(x - 4)^2 + (y - 5)^2 = 4$

____ 5. $(x + 7)^2 + (y - 2)^2 = 9$

____ 6. $x^2 - 10x + y^2 - 8y = -39$

____ 7. $x^2 + 8x + y^2 + 10y = -25$

____ 8. $x^2 - 4x + y^2 + 14y = -50$

A center: $(-7, 2)$; radius 3

B center: $(-7, -2)$; radius $\sqrt{3}$

C center: $(-2, 7)$; radius 3

D center: $(2, -7)$; radius $\sqrt{3}$

E center: $(-4, -5)$; radius 4

F center: $(4, 5)$; radius 2

G center: $(5, -4)$; radius $\sqrt{2}$

H center: $(5, 4)$; radius $\sqrt{2}$

Match each number with its equivalent form.

Using the list of numbers at the right, write the equivalent form of each given number.

4. $-\sqrt{8}$ [____]

5. $\sqrt{-8^2}$ [____]

6. $\sqrt[3]{-8}$ [____]

7. $\sqrt{-8}$ [____]

8. $\sqrt{-800}$ [____]

| -8 |
| -2 |
| $-2\sqrt{2}$ |
| $-20\sqrt{2}$ |
| $-2i$ |
| $8i$ |
| $2i\sqrt{2}$ |
| $20i\sqrt{2}$ |

On a practice test in this book, you would write either the letter of an answer choice or the answer choice itself next to each given object. For an online test, you might use drag and drop to move an answer choice next to each given object. Alternatively, you might click on both a given object and an answer choice to link them as a match.

Type of Item in *Getting Ready for High-Stakes Assessment*	What Your Online Experience May Be Like
Numerical/Algebraic Response (a type of constructed response): You produce a numerical or algebraic answer. Example: 11. a. Find sin *A* in the triangle below. 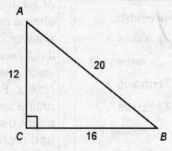 b. Write a different trigonometric ratio with the same value as sin *A*. _____ 4. Find the inverse of $f(x) = \frac{1}{2}\sqrt[3]{x+4} - 5$. Show your work. _____ _____ _____ _____ _____	On a practice test in this book, you write your answer, and you may be asked to show your work, explain your reasoning, or draw a conclusion from your answer. For an online test, you would likely be presented with an input box where you type your answer. If the answer requires the use of mathematical symbols or formatting not available on a computer keyboard, the input box would be accompanied by a palette of symbols and formatting templates that you can use as you type your answer. For a simple input box, you would type just the answer and not show work, explain reasoning, or draw a conclusion.

Type of Item in *Getting Ready for High-Stakes Assessment*	What Your Online Experience May Be Like
Graphical Response (a type of constructed response): You create some type of drawing, such as a function's graph, a data display, or a geometric figure. Examples: 5. Julius is flying home to Los Angeles from Boston. His distance away from home in miles d can be expressed in terms of t hours by the equation $d = 2600 - 500t$. Graph Julius's distance away from home in miles d after t hours, choosing appropriate scales. 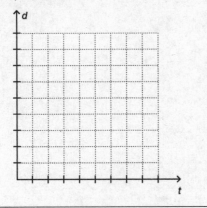 5. The data below are the average annual starting salaries (in thousands of dollars) of 20 randomly selected college graduates. Make a dot plot of the data values. 42 37 40 37 45 39 43 47 36 34 40 43 42 40 37 44 36 46 39 35 ⟵+++++++++++++++++++++++++⟶	On a practice test in this book, you draw by hand using the provided number line, coordinate plane, or starting figure. For an online test, there are a variety of ways to create drawings depending on the type of drawing: • For graphs that consist of isolated points on a number line or coordinate plane, you might plot the points simply by clicking on the number line or coordinate plane. • For more sophisticated graphs, you might use drawing tools, such as a line-drawing tool that requires you to click on two points in a coordinate plane, with the tool automatically drawing the line through those points. • For geometric figures such as polygons, you might use a connect-consecutive-points tool that automatically draws a line segment between the last point clicked and the next point clicked. • For bar graphs and histograms, you might be given bars with, say, a height of 1, and you adjust the height of a bar by clicking on the top of the bar and dragging either up or down.

Type of Item in *Getting Ready for High-Stakes Assessment*	What Your Online Experience May Be Like

Extended Response/Performance Task (a type of constructed response): You solve a multistep problem.
 	
Examples:
 	
8. A picture frame hangs on a wall as shown. The wall is 22 feet wide and 9 feet high. The square picture is 6 feet wide and its left corner is 2 feet to the right of the centerline of the wall.
 	
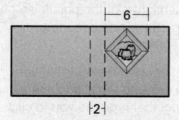
 	
  a. Suppose the lower-left corner of the wall is (0, 0) and the centerline of the wall is the line $x = 11$. Give the coordinates of the corners of the picture frame.
 	
  b. You want to locate a congruent picture frame on the left so that the two picture frames will be symmetric across the centerline of the wall. What transformation can you apply to the first picture frame to locate the second picture frame?
 	
  c. Give the coordinates of the corners of the second picture frame.
 	
  d. Describe a transformation rule using coordinate notation for a reflection across $x = 11$, the centerline of the wall. Explain how you find the transformation rule and confirm it by showing how the rule affects the four corners of the first picture frame. $(x, y) \rightarrow (?, ?)$
	On a practice test in this book, you write your answers to lettered parts of a problem, and in at least one of the parts you are asked to show your work, explain your reasoning, or draw conclusions from your answers. For an online test, you would likely be presented with one or more large response boxes. A response box allows to you type lengthy answers and may come with options for formatting text and inserting mathematical symbols.

The student will extend properties of integer exponents to rational exponents and write radicals as rational exponents.

SELECTED RESPONSE

Select the correct answer.

1. Write the radical expression in rational exponent form.

   $\sqrt[5]{a}$

   (A) a^5

   (B) $a^{\frac{1}{5}}$

   (C) 5^a

   (D) $\left(\dfrac{1}{5}\right)^a$

2. Write the radical expression in rational exponent form.

   $\sqrt[3]{k^7}$

   (A) $k^{\frac{7}{3}}$

   (B) $k^{\frac{3}{7}}$

   (C) k^4

   (D) k^{10}

3. Which values of p give the expression $p^{\frac{3}{2}}$ a real number result when simplified?

   (A) $p \geq 3$

   (B) $p \leq 2$

   (C) $p \leq 0$

   (D) $p \geq 0$

Select all correct answers.

4. Which of the following do not have integer exponents when rewritten in rational exponent form and simplified? Assume that s is nonnegative.

   (A) $\sqrt{s^4}$

   (B) $\sqrt[6]{s^3}$

   (C) $\sqrt[4]{s^6}$

   (D) $\sqrt[3]{s^9}$

   (E) $\sqrt[5]{s^{15}}$

   (F) $\sqrt[8]{s^2}$

Match each radical expression with its equivalent rational exponent expression. Assume that w is nonnegative.

_____ 5. $\sqrt[3]{w^5}$

_____ 6. $\sqrt[5]{w^3}$

_____ 7. $\sqrt{w^5}$

_____ 8. $\sqrt[3]{w}$

A $w^{\frac{5}{3}}$

B $w^{\frac{3}{5}}$

C $w^{\frac{1}{5}}$

D $w^{\frac{1}{3}}$

E $w^{\frac{2}{5}}$

F $w^{\frac{2}{3}}$

G $w^{\frac{5}{2}}$

H $w^{\frac{3}{2}}$

9. Given that the fourth root of x is defined as a quantity that, when raised to the fourth power, equals x, explain why it makes sense that $\sqrt[4]{b} = b^{\frac{1}{4}}$.

_____

_____

_____

_____

_____

_____

10. Let $n = 4m$. Rewrite $\sqrt[3n]{a^{2m}}$ in rational exponent form and simplify. Assume that m is positive.

_____

_____

_____

_____

11. Given that the definition of the cube root of x is that it's a quantity that, when raised to the third power, equals x, explain why it makes sense that $\sqrt[3]{x^4} = x^{\frac{4}{3}}$.

_____

_____

_____

_____

_____

12. A student wrote the following:
$$\sqrt[4]{x^2} = x^{\frac{2}{4}} = x^{\frac{1}{2}} = \sqrt{x}$$
Based on this, the student claims that $\sqrt[4]{x^2} = \sqrt{x}$ for all values of x.

a. Give an example of a value of x that makes this statement untrue and explain your reasoning.

_____

_____

_____

_____

_____

_____

_____

_____

_____

_____

_____

_____

b. Explain how you can restrict the value of x so that the student's statement is true.

_____

_____

_____

_____

_____

Name _____ Date _____ Class_____

The student will rewrite expressions involving radicals and rational exponents using the properties of exponents.

SELECTED RESPONSE

Select the correct answer.

1. Simplify $\left(\sqrt[7]{z^3}\right)^8$. Assume z is positive.

   (A) $z^{\frac{56}{3}}$

   (B) $z^{\frac{24}{7}}$

   (C) $z^{\frac{24}{56}}$

   (D) $z^{\frac{11}{15}}$

2. Which of the following is equal to $\sqrt[15]{\left(j^{-3}\right)^{-2}}$? Assume that j is positive.

   (A) $j^{-\frac{2}{5}}$

   (B) $j^{-\frac{1}{3}}$

   (C) $j^{\frac{5}{2}}$

   (D) $j^{\frac{2}{5}}$

3. Write $\left(\sqrt{uv^3}\right)^5$ using rational exponents. Assume u and v are both positive.

   (A) $u^{\frac{5}{2}}v^{\frac{15}{2}}$ (C) $u^{\frac{2}{5}}v^{\frac{2}{15}}$

   (B) u^5v^{15} (D) $u^{\frac{11}{2}}v^{\frac{13}{2}}$

Select all correct answers.

4. Which of the following are equal to $\left(p^{-3}\right)^{\frac{2}{5}}$? Assume that p is positive.

   (A) $\sqrt[5]{p^{-6}}$ (D) $\sqrt[5]{p^{-13}}$

   (B) $\dfrac{1}{\sqrt{p^{15}}}$ (E) $\dfrac{1}{p\sqrt[5]{p}}$

   (C) $\dfrac{1}{p^{30}}$ (F) $\sqrt[10]{p^{-1}}$

CONSTRUCTED RESPONSE

5. Write $\left(c^{-9}d^{12}\right)^{-\frac{5}{6}}$ using only positive exponents. Assume c and d are both positive. Show all work.

   _____

   _____

   _____

   _____

   _____

   _____

   _____

6. Write the four expressions in descending order of resulting exponent when written in simplified rational exponent form. Assume t is positive.

   $$\sqrt[6]{t}\cdot\sqrt[8]{t} \qquad \frac{t}{t^{\frac{5}{7}}} \qquad \left(\sqrt[3]{t^2}\right)^{\frac{4}{7}} \qquad \frac{1}{t^{-\frac{2}{5}}}$$

   _____

   _____

   _____

   _____

   _____

   _____

   _____

   _____

   _____

   _____

© Houghton Mifflin Harcourt Publishing Company

Getting Ready for High-Stakes Assessment   3   Algebra 1

7. Which values of d give the expression

$$\left[\left(d^{\frac{1}{3}}\right)^{\frac{1}{7}}\right]^{\frac{1}{4}}$$ a real number result when

simplified? Explain your answer.

_____

_____

_____

_____

_____

_____

_____

8. Show that $\left(a^{-\frac{1}{m}}\right)^{-\frac{1}{n}} = \sqrt[mn]{a}$ for positive

values of m, n, and a. Then use this

information to simplify $\left[\left(jk^4\right)^{-\frac{1}{5}}\right]^{\frac{1}{3}}$ for

positive values of j and k. Show all
work.

_____

_____

_____

_____

_____

_____

_____

9. On a recent exam, Terrell was asked to

simplify $\dfrac{x^{\frac{1}{3}}}{x^{\frac{2}{5}}}$, assuming that x is not

zero. His work is shown below.

$$\frac{x^{\frac{1}{3}}}{x^{\frac{2}{5}}} = x^{\frac{1}{3} \div \frac{2}{5}}$$

$$= x^{\frac{1}{3} \cdot \frac{5}{2}}$$

$$= x^{\frac{5}{6}}$$

$$= \sqrt[6]{x^5}$$

a. What mistake did Terrell make?

_____

_____

_____

_____

b. Find the correct answer. Show your
work.

_____

_____

_____

_____

c. Are the original expression and the
expression you found in part b
equivalent when x is negative?
Explain why or why not. (Hint:
Check to see if both expressions
have real number results with
negative x.)

_____

_____

_____

_____

_____

Name _____ Date _____ Class _____

The student will determine whether sums or products of rational and/or irrational numbers are rational or irrational.

SELECTED RESPONSE
Select the correct answer.

1. Which of the following is not a rational number?

   Ⓐ The product of 2 and $0.\overline{3}$

   Ⓑ The sum of $2+\sqrt{3}$ and $5-\sqrt{3}$

   Ⓒ The sum of $\dfrac{3}{7}$ and $\dfrac{1}{2}$

   Ⓓ The product of 2 and $\sqrt{2}$

2. Which of the following is an irrational number?

   Ⓐ The sum of 3 and 0.111....

   Ⓑ The product of $2\sqrt{3}$ and width $\dfrac{1}{\sqrt{3}}$

   Ⓒ The product of $\sqrt{16}$ and $\sqrt{9}$

   Ⓓ The sum of $\sqrt{3}$ and $0.\overline{3}$

3. Which of the following shapes has an area that's a rational number?

   Ⓐ A triangle with base $\dfrac{22}{7}$ and height π

   Ⓑ A rectangle with length $\sqrt{13}$ and width $\dfrac{1}{13}$

   Ⓒ A square with side length $1.58\overline{3}$

   Ⓓ A circle with diameter 8

Select all correct answers.

4. The perimeter of the triangle below is an irrational number.

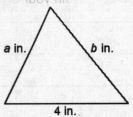

   Which of the following are possible values of a and b?

   Ⓐ $a=3+\sqrt{7},\ b=5-\sqrt{7}$

   Ⓑ $a=4,\ b=\dfrac{1}{5}$

   Ⓒ $a=\sqrt{3},\ b=5$

   Ⓓ $a=3, b=\sqrt{5}$

   Ⓔ $a=13.\overline{3},\ b=16.\overline{6}$

   Ⓕ $a=\dfrac{8}{3},\ b=\dfrac{5}{3}$

5. Indicate whether each of the following is rational or irrational by putting a check mark in the appropriate column of the table.

	Rational	Irrational
The product of $\sqrt{2}$ and 5		
$f(x)=x^2+2$ evaluated at $x=\sqrt{7}$		
The sum of $\sqrt{10}$ and $\sqrt{16}$		
$f(r)=\pi r^2$ evaluated at $r=3$		

Name _____ Date _____ Class _____

CONSTRUCTED RESPONSE

6. Classify $\left(5-\sqrt{2}\right)\left(10+\sqrt{8}\right)$ as rational or irrational. Explain your reasoning.

_____

_____

_____

_____

_____

_____

_____

7. Explain why the area of a circle with a rational radius must be an irrational number.

_____

_____

_____

_____

_____

_____

8. Given that the set of rational numbers is closed under addition, prove that the sum of a nonzero rational number and an irrational number is an irrational number.

_____

_____

_____

_____

_____

_____

_____

9. Given that the set of rational numbers is closed under multiplication, prove that the product of a nonzero rational number and an irrational number is an irrational number.

_____

_____

_____

_____

_____

_____

_____

_____

Name _____ Date _____ Class_____

The student will use units to guide solutions, choose units in formulas, and interpret the scale and origin in data displays.

SELECTED RESPONSE

1. A certain cooking oil has a density of 0.91 gram per milliliter. Using the expressions below, write the series of calculations that correctly determines the mass, in kilograms, of 15 liters of this oil.

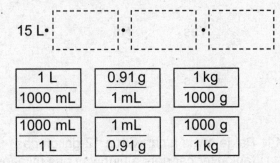

$15 \text{ L} \cdot$ [ ] $\cdot$ [ ] $\cdot$ [ ]

$\dfrac{1 \text{ L}}{1000 \text{ mL}}$	$\dfrac{0.91 \text{ g}}{1 \text{ mL}}$	$\dfrac{1 \text{ kg}}{1000 \text{ g}}$
$\dfrac{1000 \text{ mL}}{1 \text{ L}}$	$\dfrac{1 \text{ mL}}{0.91 \text{ g}}$	$\dfrac{1000 \text{ g}}{1 \text{ kg}}$

Select the correct answer.

2. Ordering n books from an online bookstore at \$19.99 per book comes with a 6.25% sales tax and a shipping charge of \$3.50 for each book after the first. If n is the whole number of books ordered, what are the units for the quantity represented by the expression $19.99n + 0.0625(19.99n) + 3.50(n - 1)$?

Ⓐ dollars

Ⓑ books

Ⓒ dollars per book

Ⓓ percent of total cost

3. Shawn jogs n blocks, each of which are d meters long, in t minutes. What are the units for the expression $\dfrac{nd}{t}$, Shawn's average speed for his jog?

Ⓐ blocks

Ⓑ meters

Ⓒ minutes

Ⓓ meters per minute

Each activity will be graphed, with time on the horizontal axis. Match the activities with appropriate scales for the horizontal axis.

_____ 4. Graphing the remaining amount of a sandwich against the time taken to eat it

_____ 5. Graphing the distance traveled against the time taken to drive to work 30 miles away during rush hour

_____ 6. Graphing the distance traveled against the time taken to fly from the east coast of the United States to the west coast

_____ 7. Graphing the amount of weight lost against the time spent on a new diet and exercise regimen

_____ 8. Graphing the length of a signature against the time spent writing it

A 0 days to 60 days

B 0 seconds to 2 seconds

C 0 minutes to 10 minutes

D 0 hours to 24 hours

E 0 hours to 10 hours

F 0 minutes to 60 minutes

G 0 seconds to 30 seconds

H 0 days to 3 days

Select the correct answer for each lettered part.

9. A newton is a unit of force, and it's measured in units of kilogram-meters per second squared, or $\frac{kg \cdot m}{s^2}$. Which of the following represent a quantity measured in newtons?

   a. $150\ g \cdot \dfrac{1\ kg}{1000\ g} \cdot \dfrac{3\ m}{s^2}$ ○ Yes   ○ No

   b. $\dfrac{7}{350\ kg} \cdot \dfrac{2\ m}{s^2}$ ○ Yes   ○ No

   c. $1.8\ kg \cdot \dfrac{25\ cm}{100\ cm} \cdot \dfrac{1\ m}{s^2}$ ○ Yes   ○ No

   d. $37\ g \cdot \dfrac{107\ mm}{s^2} \cdot \dfrac{kg}{1000\ g} \cdot \dfrac{1\ m}{1000\ mm}$ ○ Yes   ○ No

CONSTRUCTED RESPONSE

10. A local store sells muffins for $0.75 each. The graph below shows a customer's total bill C as a function of m muffins purchased, which can be represented by the function $C = 0.75m$.

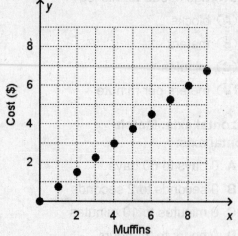

   Explain what the point at the origin represents.

   _____

   _____

   _____

11. Paige owns a car with a 12-gallon gas tank. Her car gets a highway gas mileage of 32 miles per gallon.

   a. Write two ratios to represent the gas mileage of Paige's car. Make sure to include the units for the quantities.

   _____

   b. Paige wants to drive to her sister's house, which is 162.4 highway miles away from where she lives. Use one of the ratios you wrote in part a to calculate how many gallons of gas Paige needs to make the trip.

   _____

   _____

   c. Gas costs $3.50 per gallon. Write two ratios to represent the cost of a gallon of gas. Make sure to include units for the quantities.

   _____

   d. Use one of your ratios from part c to calculate how much Paige's trip costs. Round up to the nearest cent.

   _____

   _____

The student will define appropriate quantities for the purpose of descriptive modeling.

SELECTED RESPONSE
Select the correct answer.

1. The math club is having a fundraiser, selling mugs for $5 each and T-shirts for $10 each. The club raised $1000. Which model describes the relationship between sales and money raised?

   Ⓐ $5(the number of mugs sold) + $10(the number of T-shirts sold) = $15

   Ⓑ $10(the number of mugs sold) + $5(the number of T-shirts sold) = $1000

   Ⓒ $5(the number of mugs sold) + $10(the number of T-shirts sold) = $1000

   Ⓓ $5(the number of mugs sold) − $10(the number of T-shirts sold) = $1000

2. Zach earns $10 for every lawn he rakes and $15 for every lawn he mows. He deposits $500 into his college fund at the end of the summer. Which model describes the relationship between work and money earned?

   Ⓐ $15(lawns raked) + $10(lawns mowed) = $500

   Ⓑ $10(lawns raked) + $15(lawns mowed) = $500

   Ⓒ (lawns raked) + (lawns mowed) = $500

   Ⓓ $10(lawns raked) + $15(lawns mowed) = $25

3. Susie's Clothing Store sells sweatshirts for $30 and sweatpants for $25. The Drama Club buys a total of 100 sweatshirts and sweatpants and spends $2825. Which model describes this situation?

   Ⓐ $\begin{cases} \$30(\text{the number of sweatshirts}) + \$25(\text{the number of sweatpants}) = \$2825 \\ \text{the number of sweatshirts} + \text{the number of sweatpants} = 100 \end{cases}$

   Ⓑ $\begin{cases} \$30(\text{the number of sweatshirts}) + \$25(\text{the number of sweatpants}) = \$2825 \\ \text{the number of sweatshirts} - \text{the number of sweatpants} = 100 \end{cases}$

   Ⓒ $\begin{cases} \$25(\text{the number of sweatshirts}) + \$30(\text{the number of sweatpants}) = \$2825 \\ \text{the number of sweatshirts} + \text{the number of sweatpants} = 100 \end{cases}$

   Ⓓ $\begin{cases} \$30(\text{the number of sweatshirts}) + \$30(\text{the number of sweatpants}) = \$2825 \\ \$25(\text{the number of sweatshirts}) + \$25(\text{the number of sweatpants}) = \$2825 \end{cases}$

Match each situation with the correct expression.

Using the list of expressions on the right, write the expression that models the given description of the growth of a culture of bacteria cells. Assume that the culture begins with a single cell and that t represents time in hours.

4. The cell count doubles every hour: [ ]

5. The culture produces three more cells every hour: [ ]

6. The cell count triples every hour: [ ]

$t + 2$
3^t
$(t + 1)^2$
2^t
$t + 3$
$3t + 1$

CONSTRUCTED RESPONSE

7. A factory produces widgets and sprockets. The factory sells widgets for $2 each, and sprockets for $3 each. The total amount of money earned from selling widgets and sprockets last month was $3000.

   a. Choose appropriate variables to represent the number of widgets sold and the number of sprockets sold. Write an equation representing the total amount of money earned from selling widgets and sprockets.

   _____

   _____

   _____

   b. Write an appropriate model for the situation in which this factory sold 1225 widgets and sprockets to earn $3000.

   _____

   _____

   _____

   _____

   c. This factory also sells gizmos for $5. Choose an appropriate variable to represent the number of gizmos sold and write an equation representing the situation in which the total amount of money earned from selling widgets, sprockets, and gizmos is $5000.

   _____

   _____

   _____

8. A model rocket's height after being launched is modeled by a quadratic function.

   a. One quantity of interest is maximum height. What other quantity might be of interest?

   _____

   b. The maximum height of the rocket's flight path is 192 meters after 8 seconds. Find and choose the dependent and independent variables that represent the quantities in this problem. Include units.

   _____

   _____

   _____

   c. Write a function that models the height of the rocket as it relates to the time since the rocket was launched, given that the rocket starts at a height of 0. Write the function in the form $f(x) = a(x-h)^2 + k$.

   _____

   _____

   _____

   d. This rocket is being fired off in a certain town. In the interest of safety, town regulations dictate that model rockets should land no more than 20 meters from where they are launched. This rocket's horizontal speed during flight is 1.5 meters per second. Does this rocket meet local regulations? Explain your reasoning.

   _____

   _____

   _____

The student will choose a level of accuracy appropriate to limitations on measurement when reporting quantities.

SELECTED RESPONSE
Select the correct answer.

1. A triangle has side lengths 2.02 cm, 3.570 cm, and 4.1 cm. What is the perimeter of this triangle to the correct number of significant digits?

   Ⓐ 9.69

   Ⓑ 9.690

   Ⓒ 9.7

   Ⓓ 10

2. Which of these measurements is the most precise?

   Ⓐ 4 m

   Ⓑ 127 mm

   Ⓒ 1.3 km

   Ⓓ 5.14 cm

3. A rectangle has a length of 4.2 feet and a width of 7.36 feet. How many significant digits does the area of the rectangle have?

   Ⓐ 2   Ⓒ 5

   Ⓑ 3   Ⓓ 6

Select all correct answers.

4. Which of the following calculated values will have three significant digits?

   Ⓐ The perimeter of a square with side length 1.02 ft

   Ⓑ The area of a square with side length 0.024 m

   Ⓒ The perimeter of a triangle with side lengths 84.5 cm, 94 cm, and 117 cm

   Ⓓ The area of a triangle with base 4.50 in. and height 10.02 in.

   Ⓔ The circumference of a circle with radius 0.0910 m

   Ⓕ The area of a circle with radius 5000 ft

5. Indicate by putting a check mark in the appropriate column of the table whether each measurement has more, fewer, or the same number of significant digits as the volume of a cube with side length 14.20 feet.

	More	Fewer	Same
The surface area of a sphere with radius 4.2 m			
The sum of dimensions 2.049 ft and 10.67 ft			
Half of the length 175.08 m			
The sum of lengths 12.125 mm and 10 mm			
The product of 120.7 cm, 44.50 cm, and 1.553 cm			

Name _____ Date _____ Class _____

CONSTRUCTED RESPONSE

6. Do 38,000 cm, 38 cm, 0.038 cm, and 0.00038 cm all have the same number of significant digits? Explain your reasoning, including the number of significant digits in each measurement.

_____

_____

_____

_____

7. A company produces parts for an automobile manufacturer. One part consists of two rods connected end to end with a joint. The lengths for the rods are 31.4 cm and 82.25 cm.

   a. What is the combined length of the two rods, using the correct number of significant digits? (Assume that the joint doesn't add any additional length.) Show your work.

   _____

   _____

   _____

   b. The automobile company says that the combined length of the two rods must be within 0.01 cm of 113.65 cm. The manager of the company says that this level of precision isn't possible given the precision of the lengths of the individual parts. Is the manager correct? Explain why or why not.

   _____

   _____

8. Two physics classes at two different schools have a competition to build the best catapult. Each class will throw rubber balls with the same weight, and both will use a tape measure marked in eighths of an inch to measure the results.

   At his school, Randal fires his catapult and measures the distance it throws the ball. The edge of the ball falls between the marks for 13 feet $10\frac{1}{8}$ inches and 13 feet $10\frac{1}{4}$ inches, so he rounds to the eighth of an inch closest to where his ball landed, which is 13 feet $10\frac{1}{8}$ inches. At her school, Lacey fires her catapult and measures the distance. Her distance falls between the same two marks, but she reports her distance as 13 feet $10\frac{3}{16}$ inches and claims she's won.

   a. What measurement error did Lacey make?

   _____

   _____

   b. The judges declare a tie, but is it possible that Randal would have won if they used a measuring tape with higher precision? Explain why or why not.

   _____

   _____

   _____

   _____

   _____

© Houghton Mifflin Harcourt Publishing Company

Getting Ready for High-Stakes Assessment   12   Algebra 1

The student will interpret parts of an expression, such as terms, factors, and coefficients.

SELECTED RESPONSE

Select the correct answer.

1. A clothing store is having a sale in which all T-shirts are $10. The sales tax is 5%. If Dan buys *n* T-shirts during this sale, the total cost of his purchase will be $10n + 0.05(10n)$. Interpret the meaning of $0.05(10n)$ in this context.

   Ⓐ The expression $0.05(10n)$ represents the price of each T-shirt.

   Ⓑ The expression $0.05(10n)$ represents the cost of Dan's purchase before tax.

   Ⓒ The expression $0.05(10n)$ represents the total tax on Dan's purchase.

   Ⓓ The expression $0.05(10n)$ represents the total cost of Dan's purchase.

2. A painter working high on the side of a skyscraper drops his brush from his scaffolding, which is hanging 1024 feet above the ground. The height above the ground of the brush can be modeled by the equation $h = -16t^2 + 1024$, where *t* is the number of seconds after the brush is dropped and *h* is the height in feet. Interpret the meaning of $-16t^2$ in this context.

   Ⓐ The term $-16t^2$ represents the time the brush takes to hit the ground.

   Ⓑ The term $-16t^2$ represents the initial height of the brush.

   Ⓒ The term $-16t^2$ represents the height of the brush after *t* seconds.

   Ⓓ The term $-16t^2$ represents the distance the brush falls in *t* seconds.

3. A bacteria culture starts with three cells. Each cell in this culture doubles every hour. After *t* hours, the number of cells in the culture can be written as $3(2^t)$. Interpret the meaning of 2^t in this context.

   Ⓐ The factor 2^t is the initial number of cells.

   Ⓑ The factor 2^t is the number of hours.

   Ⓒ The factor 2^t is the number of cells in the culture after *t* hours.

   Ⓓ The factor 2^t is the number of cells that each original cell in the culture has produced after *t* hours.

Select all correct answers.

4. A theme park costs $25.00 to enter. One of the food stands within the park sells hot dogs for $2.50 each and hamburgers for $3.50 each. If Paul enters the park, walks to the food stand, and purchases *d* hot dogs and *b* hamburgers, the amount of money *m* he spends can be modeled by the equation $m = 2.5d + 3.5b + 25$. Circle each statement that is a correct interpretation of a part of this equation.

   The cost of entering the park is 2.5*d*.

   The cost of entering the park is 25.

   The cost of entering the park is 3.5*b*.

   The cost of purchasing *d* hot dogs is 2.5*d*.

   The cost of purchasing *b* hot dogs is 3.5*b*.

   The cost of purchasing *d* hamburgers is 2.5*d*.

   The cost of purchasing *b* hamburgers is 3.5*b*.

   The cost of purchasing *d* hot dogs and *b* hamburgers is 25.

Name _____ Date _____ Class _____

CONSTRUCTED RESPONSE

5. A certain vine grows at a rate of three inches per day. A researcher starts observing it when it is 27 inches long.

   a. Write an algebraic expression for the length, in feet, of the vine d days after the researcher starts observing it.

   _____

   b. Interpret both of the factors in the variable term.

   _____
   _____
   _____
   _____
   _____

   c. Interpret the variable term.

   _____
   _____
   _____
   _____

6. A full fifty-gallon tank of water has a small leak. Two gallons of water are lost through this leak every day. Write an algebraic expression for the amount of water, in gallons, in the tank after d days and interpret any coefficients in the expression, as well as any variables being multiplied by those coefficients.

   _____
   _____
   _____

7. The volume of a composite figure is $s^3 + (0.5s)^2 \pi h$.

   a. Interpret what s, s^3, $0.5s$, and $(0.5s)^2 \pi h$ could each represent.

   _____
   _____
   _____
   _____
   _____

   b. Sketch the figure.

8. Part of the water in a pond in a local park was covered by 4 ft^2 of algae. Local residents who frequented the park noticed the area of the pond covered by algae tripled every week. Write an algebraic expression for the area of algae covering the pond after w weeks and interpret the factors of the expression.

   _____
   _____
   _____
   _____
   _____

The student will interpret complicated expressions by viewing one or more of their parts as a single entity.

SELECTED RESPONSE
Select the correct answer.

1. Students at a bake sale sell bags of cookies for $2.25 each and bags of miniature muffins for $1.50 each. While selling their baked goods, the students also received a $25 donation. The amount of money the students make from selling c bags of cookies and m bags of muffins can be modeled by the expression $2.25c + 1.5m + 25$. Interpret the expression $2.25c + 1.5m$ in this context.

   Ⓐ The expression $2.25c + 1.5m$ represents the money earned from selling c bags of cookies.

   Ⓑ The expression $2.25c + 1.5m$ represents the money earned from selling m bags of muffins.

   Ⓒ The expression $2.25c + 1.5m$ represents the money earned from selling c bags of cookies and m bags of muffins.

   Ⓓ The expression $2.25c + 1.5m$ represents the money earned from selling one bag of cookies and one bag of muffins.

2. Tatiana deposits $500 into a bank account that pays 3.25% interest compounded annually. The expression $(1 + 0.0325)^t$ represents the number of dollars in the account after t years for every dollar in the original balance. Which of the following is a reasonable interpretation of the expression $500(1 + 0.0325)^t$ in this context?

   Ⓐ The amount of interest the account earns after 1 year

   Ⓑ The amount of interest the account earns after 500 years

   Ⓒ The amount of money in the account after 1 year

   Ⓓ The amount of money in the account after t years

3. A store is roping off a rectangular area of the floor that needs some repairs. The staff uses 36 feet of rope. Given w is the width of the roped-off floor in feet, write words from the list below to complete the sentence.

   The ⌐ ‾ ‾ ‾ ¬ of the roped-off
         ⌞ _ _ _ ⌟

   floor in ⌐ ‾ ‾ ‾ ¬ is represented
            ⌞ _ _ _ ⌟

   by the expression $\dfrac{18 - w}{3}$.

width	length	perimeter
area	yards	square yards

Select all correct answers.

4. Which of the following scenarios give reasonable interpretations of $(1 + 0.05)^t$ in the expression $250(1 + 0.05)^t$?

   Ⓐ Marisa deposits $250 into a bank account that pays 5% interest compounded annually. After t years, she will have $(1 + 0.05)^t$ dollars in the account.

   Ⓑ A snake is 250 mm long. It increases in length by 5% every week. After t weeks the snake will be $(1 + 0.05)^t$ times longer.

   Ⓒ A cell culture has 250 cells, and the population of cells grows at a rate of 5% per day. There were $(1 + 0.05)^t$ cells when the culture first started to grow.

   Ⓓ A sinkhole is 250 feet deep. Every year, it becomes 5% deeper. After t years, the sinkhole is $(1 + 0.05)^t$ feet deeper.

   Ⓔ An empty water tank is partially filled with 250 gallons, and the volume of water in the tank increases by 5% each month afterward. After t months, the number of gallons will be increased by a factor of $(1 + 0.05)^t$.

Match each situation with the correct expression.

A local supermarket has a section that serves ready-to-eat food in a buffet style. The section consists of a salad bar, an olive bar, and a wings bar. The salad bar costs $3.99/lb, the olive bar costs $6.49/lb, and the wings bar costs $4.99/lb. Let d be the number of pounds of salad purchased, v the number of pounds of olives, and w the number of pounds of wings. Match the algebraic expressions with their appropriate interpretations in this context.

_____ 5. $6.49v + 4.99w$

_____ 6. $0.80(3.99d + 4.99w)$

_____ 7. $3.99d$

_____ 8. $\dfrac{3.99d + 6.49v}{3}$.

A The cost of three people purchasing d pounds of salad

B The cost of purchasing d pounds of salad and w pounds of wings, using a 20% off coupon

C The cost per person if three people split d pounds of salad and v pounds of olives

D The cost of purchasing d pounds of salad and v pounds of olives

E The cost of purchasing d pounds of salad and w pounds of wings

F The cost of purchasing d pounds of salad

G The cost of purchasing v pounds of olives and w pounds of wings

CONSTRUCTED RESPONSE

9. A minor league baseball team wants to sell ad space on their outfield wall to local businesses. The team originally thinks about charging $250 per ad. However, the local businesses know that the more ads there are, the less focus each individual ad will get, so they're not willing to pay as much per ad if they know there will be more of them. The team does market research and finds that they can get $250 for one ad, $245 per ad for two ads, $240 per ad for three ads, and so on. The total revenue from all the outfield banners is calculated using the expression $a(250 - 5(a - 1))$. Interpret what the expression $250 - 5(a - 1)$ represents, and explain your reasoning.

_____

_____

_____

10. Each day, a plant grows to a height that is 20% taller than it was the previous day. The expression $(1 + 0.20)^d$ represents the plant's height after d days if its original height is 1 inch. Another plant with the same growth rate is described by the expression $1.75(1 + 0.20)^d$. Interpret 1.75 in this expression and use this to interpret the entire expression.

_____

_____

_____

The student will use the structure of an expression to identify ways to rewrite it.

SELECTED RESPONSE

Select the correct answer.

1. Which of the following is equal to $x^6 - 64$?

   Ⓐ $-64x^6$

   Ⓑ $(x^3 + 8)(x^3 - 8)$

   Ⓒ $(x^3 + 8)^2$

   Ⓓ $(x^3 - 8)^2$

2. What value of a will make the following statement true?
   $$5^{3(x-2)} = a5^{3x}$$

   Ⓐ 5^2

   Ⓑ $\dfrac{1}{5^2}$

   Ⓒ 5^6

   Ⓓ $\dfrac{1}{5^6}$

3. If Jan jogged $8x - 21$ miles and Julie jogged $24x - 63$ miles, how many times longer was Julie's travel distance than Jan's?

   Ⓐ 3

   Ⓑ 16

   Ⓒ 24

   Ⓓ 63

Select all correct answers.

4. Circle each expression that can be rewritten as a sum of cubes, a difference of cubes, or a difference of squares.

   $81 - x^4$ $n^6 + 64$

   $y^5 - 9$ $25 - 4c^{16}$

   $5p^3 + 27$ $216 - t^{18}$

5. Which of the following statements present(s) valid reasoning?

   Ⓐ $x^6 + 81$ can be rewritten as $(x^2)^3 + (3)^3$ and factored as a sum of two cubes.

   Ⓑ $49c^2 - 154c + 121$ can be rewritten as $(7c)^2 - 2(7c)(11) + 11^2$ and factored as a perfect square trinomial.

   Ⓒ $36p^4 + 96p + 64$ can be rewritten as $(6p^2)^2 + 2(6p^2)(8) + 8^2$ and factored as a perfect square trinomial.

   Ⓓ $x^4 + 16$ can be rewritten as $(x^2)^2 - (-4)^2$ and factored as a difference of squares.

   Ⓔ $x^{18} - 8$ can be rewritten as $(x^6)^3 - 2^3$ and factored as a difference of cubes.

   Ⓕ $x^9 + 64$ cannot be factored as the sum of two cubes because x^9 is a perfect cube and 64 is a perfect square.

CONSTRUCTED RESPONSE

6. How many binomials can $6561 - 256y^{16}$ be factored into before it is factored completely? Show your work. (Hint: 6561 is 3 raised to a power.)

   _____

   _____

   _____

   _____

   _____

   _____

   _____

   _____

   _____

   _____

7. a. Rewrite $9k^4 + 78k^2 + 169$ in the form $a^2 + 2ab + b^2$.

    _____

    _____

    b. Factor your answer to part a using the formula $(a + b)^2 = a^2 + 2ab + b^2$.

    _____

    _____

    _____

8. Al and Tim each have rectangular wooden decks on their homes. Al's deck is 4 feet wide and has area $60x + 40$ ft^2. Tim's deck is 7 feet wide and has area $21x + 14$ ft^2. Determine an expression for the length of each deck. How many times the length of Tim's deck is Al's deck? Show your work.

    _____

    _____

    _____

    _____

    _____

    _____

    _____

    _____

    _____

    _____

    _____

    _____

9. a. Are there values of a and b such that $25x^2 + 90x + 81 = (ax + b)^2$? Explain. (Hint: Expand $(ax + b)^2$ and try to find values of a and b that satisfy the equation.)

    _____

    _____

    _____

    _____

    _____

    _____

    _____

    _____

    _____

    _____

    b. Are there values of a and b such that $9y^4 + 30y^2 + 49 = (ay^2 + b)^2$? Explain.

    _____

    _____

    _____

    _____

    _____

    _____

    _____

    _____

    _____

    _____

    _____

    _____

The student will factor a quadratic expression to reveal the zeros of the function it defines.

SELECTED RESPONSE
Select the correct answer.

1. After factoring a quadratic expression that equals zero, which property says that at least one of the factors must equal zero?

   Ⓐ The Distributive Property

   Ⓑ The Zero Product Property

   Ⓒ The Additive Property of Equality

   Ⓓ The Multiplicative Property of Equality

Select all correct answers.

2. Circle each function that has at least one zero greater than 4.

   $w(c) = c^2 + 11c + 30$ $v(a) = a^2 - 5a + 6$

   $f(x) = x^2 - 5x - 14$ $s(t) = t^2 - 3t - 54$

   $g(x) = x^2 + 5x - 24$ $h(x) = x^2 - 2x - 24$

Factor each quadratic function and match it with the correct description of its zeros.

____ 3. $s(r) = 5r^2 + 49r - 10$

____ 4. $k(m) = m^2 - 7m - 18$

____ 5. $z(w) = w^2 + 7w + 6$

____ 6. $f(x) = 2x^2 - 11x + 12$

A One positive zero

B One negative zero

C One positive zero and one negative zero, where the positive zero has the larger absolute value

D Two positive zeros

E Two negative zeros

F One positive zero and one negative zero, where the negative zero has the larger absolute value

CONSTRUCTED RESPONSE

7. Identify the zero(s) of $m(n) = n^2 - 23n + 132$ by factoring. Show your work.

   _____

   _____

8. Identify the zero(s) of $f(x) = 3x^2 + 8x - 35$ by factoring. Show your work.

   _____

   _____

9. If $f(x) = x^2 + bx + c$ has two zeros and $c < 0$, explain how you know that one zero must be positive and one zero must be negative.

   _____

   _____

   _____

   _____

10. A catapult is used to launch a boulder. The height of the boulder $h(t)$ can be modeled by the function $h(t) = -16t^2 + 64t$, where t is the time in seconds after the boulder is launched. Assuming that the boulder doesn't hit anything, how many seconds after launch will the boulder hit the ground? Show your work.

_____

_____

_____

_____

_____

_____

11. For a publicity stunt, a radio station has a basketball trick shot artist throw a basketball from a studio window to a hoop below. The height of the ball above the hoop, in feet, can be modeled by the function $h(t) = -16t^2 + 4t + 240$, where t is the time in seconds after the ball is thrown. How long after the ball is thrown does it pass through the hoop? Show your work.

_____

_____

_____

_____

_____

_____

12. Assume $f(x) = x^2 + bx + c$ has two zeros, $b > 0$, and $c < 0$.

   a. What can you conclude about the signs of the two zeros of the function? Explain your reasoning.

   _____

   _____

   _____

   _____

   _____

   _____

   b. What can you conclude about the absolute values of the two zeros? Explain your reasoning.

   _____

   _____

   _____

   _____

   _____

   _____

   c. If $b < 0$, how does this change the conclusions from parts a and b? Explain your reasoning.

   _____

   _____

   _____

   _____

   _____

   _____

Name _____ Date _____ Class_____

The student will complete the square in a quadratic expression to reveal the maximum or minimum value of the function it defines.

SELECTED RESPONSE
Select the correct answer.

1. In which quadrant does the minimum of $f(x) = x^2 - 3x - 1$ occur?

   Ⓐ Quadrant I

   Ⓑ Quadrant II

   Ⓒ Quadrant III

   Ⓓ Quadrant IV

2. Which of the following is a true statement about the function $f(x) = x^2 + 5x + 5$?

   Ⓐ The maximum of the function is $-\dfrac{5}{4}$.

   Ⓑ The minimum of the function is $-\dfrac{5}{4}$.

   Ⓒ The maximum of the function is $-\dfrac{5}{2}$.

   Ⓓ The minimum of the function is $-\dfrac{5}{2}$.

Select all correct answers.

3. Determine which functions have a minimum value that is greater than zero.

   Ⓐ $f(x) = x^2 - 6x + 5$

   Ⓑ $f(x) = x^2 + 4x + 7$

   Ⓒ $f(t) = t^2 + 8t - 10$

   Ⓓ $f(n) = n^2 + 10n + 11$

   Ⓔ $f(p) = p^2 - 2p + 8$

4. Indicate by putting a check mark in the appropriate column of the table whether the maximum value of each function is greater than or less than 7.

	Less	Greater
$f(x) = -4x^2 + 6x + 5$		
$g(c) = -c^2 + 9c - 15$		
$f(t) = -4t^2 + 11t - 3$		
$g(t) = -9t^2 - 21t - 4$		

CONSTRUCTED RESPONSE

5. Complete the square to find the maximum value of $f(x) = -x^2 + 7x - 11$. Show your work.

   _____

   _____

   _____

   _____

   _____

   _____

6. Complete the square to find the minimum value of $f(x) = 2x^2 - 5x + 7$. Show your work.

   _____

   _____

   _____

   _____

   _____

   _____

7. Explain why $f(x) = 4x^2 + 5x + c$ has a greater minimum than $g(x) = 9x^2 + 10x + c$ regardless of the value of c.

   _____

   _____

   _____

   _____

   _____

   _____

   _____

8. A game store sells a brand of playing cards for $10. On average, the store sells 100 of these decks per year. The store manager considers raising the price of the decks. The manager expects that for every $1 increase in price, the store will sell 4 fewer decks per year.

   a. Write a function for the gross yearly revenue the manager expects to earn from selling this brand of card deck after x $1 price increases.

     _____

     _____

   b. Complete the square to determine the maximum yearly revenue the store could earn from selling this brand. Show your work.

     _____

     _____

     _____

     _____

     _____

     _____

   c. For how much should the store sell the card decks to earn the maximum yearly revenue? Show your work.

     _____

     _____

     _____

     _____

     _____

9. A ball is thrown up into the air. Its height h above the ground in feet is modeled by the equation $h = -16t^2 + 24t + 5$, where t is the time in seconds after the ball is thrown. Complete the square to determine the ball's maximum height and the amount of time the ball takes to reach that height. Could this ball land on the roof of a 20-foot-tall building? Show your work.

_____

_____

_____

_____

_____

_____

_____

_____

_____

_____

_____

_____

_____

_____

_____

_____

_____

_____

_____

_____

The student will use the properties of exponents to transform expressions for exponential functions.

SELECTED RESPONSE
Select the correct answer.

1. Which of the following is equivalent to the expression $81 \cdot 9^{x+2}$?

   (A) 81^{x+1}

   (B) 9^{2x+4}

   (C) 6561^x

   (D) 3^{2x+8}

2. Which of the following cannot be rewritten in the form $f(x) = 2^{ax}$, where a is an integer?

   (A) $f(x) = 4^{bx}$, where b is an integer

   (B) $f(x) = 8^{bx}$, where b is an integer

   (C) $f(x) = 12^{bx}$, where b is an integer

   (D) $f(x) = 16^{bx}$, where b is an integer

3. A certain radioactive element has a half-life of 35 days. If you had 100 grams of this element, the mass m of the element after t 35-day intervals is represented by $m = 100(0.5)^t$. Find the approximate daily decay rate of this element.

   (A) 98.0%

   (B) 17.5%

   (C) 2.0%

   (D) 1.4%

Select all correct answers.

4. Which of the following are equivalent to $f(x) = 16^x$?

   (A) $g(x) = 8 \cdot 2^x$

   (B) $g(x) = 4096 \cdot 16^{x-3}$

   (C) $g(x) = 4 \cdot 4^x$

   (D) $g(x) = 0.0625 \cdot 16^{x+1}$

   (E) $g(x) = 32 \cdot 16^{x-2}$

   (F) $g(x) = 2 \cdot 8^x$

5. Select from the numbers below to rewrite $f(x) = 625^{2x}$.

   $f(x) = \boxed{}^{\boxed{}x}$

   | 5 | 2 | 4 | 8 | 10 |

CONSTRUCTED RESPONSE

6. How many times greater are the values of the function $g(x) = 3^{x+2}$ than the values of the function $f(x) = 3^x$ for all values of x? Show your work.

   _____

   _____

   _____

   _____

   _____

7. A certain culture contains 8 bacteria cells. The cell population of the culture doubles in size every hour.

   a. Write a function in the form $f(t) = a \cdot b^t$ for the number of cells in the culture after t hours.

   _____

   _____

   b. Write a function $g(t) = d^{pt+q}$ that is equivalent to $f(t)$, where p and q are non-zero integers. Show algebraically that this new function is equivalent to $f(t)$.

   _____

   _____

   _____

   _____

8. A certain debt of $7000 must be repaid with 20% interest compounded annually. The value of the debt D after t years is represented by $D = 7000(1.2)^t$.

   a. Rewrite this function to determine the approximate monthly interest rate of the debt. Show your work and round percent answers to one decimal place.

   _____

   _____

   _____

   _____

   b. Rewrite the function from part a to find the approximate bimonthly (every two months) interest rate of the debt. Show your work and round percent answers to one decimal place.

   _____

   _____

   _____

   _____

   c. Rewrite the function from part a to find the semiannual interest rate of the debt. Show your work and round percent answers to one decimal place.

   _____

   _____

   _____

9. What is the smallest value of n such that $f(x) = n^x$ can be rewritten as both $f(x) = 4^{ax}$ and $f(x) = 8^{bx}$, where both a and b are positive integers? Justify your answer.

   _____

   _____

   _____

   _____

   _____

   _____

   _____

   _____

   _____

   _____

   _____

   _____

   _____

   _____

   _____

   _____

   _____

   _____

   _____

   _____

   _____

   _____

The student will understand closure of polynomials under operations and will add, subtract, and multiply polynomials.

SELECTED RESPONSE
Select the correct answer.

1. Which of the following best describes the sum of $ax^2 + bx + c$ and $mx^2 + nx + p$, where x is a variable and a, b, c, m, n, and p are real numbers.

    (A) The sum is a constant.

    (B) The sum is an exponential expression.

    (C) The sum is a polynomial.

    (D) Nothing can be determined about the sum without more information.

2. If $2x^2 - 5x + 7$ is subtracted from $4x^2 + 2x - 11$, what is the coefficient of x in the result?

    (A) 2

    (B) 7

    (C) -3

    (D) -18

3. What is the resulting polynomial when $3x + 7$ is multiplied by $2x - 6$?

    (A) $5x + 1$

    (B) $6x - 42$

    (C) $6x^2 - 4x - 42$

    (D) $6x^2 + 9x - 42$

Select all correct answers.

4. Simplify each of the following expressions to determine which are linear.

    (A) $(x^2 + 6x + 9) + (x^2 - 4x + 4)$

    (B) $2(2x^2 + x - 10) - (5x^2 - 3x + 1)$

    (C) $4(3x^2 + 5x - 4) - 6(2x^2 + 2x - 1)$

    (D) $3(x^2 - x + 1) + (-2x^2 + 4x - 5)$

    (E) $4(2x^2 - 6x + 7) - 8(x^2 - 3x + 4)$

5. Simplify each expression. Indicate by putting a check mark in the appropriate column of the table whether the coefficient of x in the result is positive, negative, or zero.

	Positive	Negative	Zero
$(5x + 10) + (x - 100)$			
$\left(\frac{11}{4}x - 2\right) - \left(8x - \frac{13}{2}\right)$			
$(6.4x - 3.2)(x + 0.5)$			
$\left(-3x + 4\sqrt{5}\right) - \left(-2x - \sqrt{13}\right)$			
$(-1.7x - 4.2) + \left(\frac{20x}{7} - \sqrt{7}\right)$			

CONSTRUCTED RESPONSE

6. Write $(2x + 1)(3x - 8)$ in expanded form.

_____

_____

7. Will the simplified form of the sum of two quadratic polynomials with x^2 terms always have an x^2 term? Explain.

_____

_____

_____

_____

_____

_____

8. Wanda manages a webstore that specializes in kitchenware. The store sells a tea set for $65, and it averages 30 sales of this tea set per month. Based on past sales, Wanda estimates that for every $5 price increase for this tea set, she will sell 2 fewer sets each month. Write an expression for Wanda's monthly gross revenue from tea set sales after x $5 price increases as the product of two factors and then rewrite the expression in expanded form. Show your work.

_____

_____

_____

_____

_____

_____

_____

_____

_____

9. Two cars are driving along a straight highway at a constant speed. At a certain point in time, one car is 1.2 miles away from a landmark and is driving at 65 miles per hour, and the other car is 0.7 miles away from the same landmark and is driving at 55 miles per hour.

a. Write an expression for the distance between the first car and the landmark in terms of the number of hours spent driving t if the car is driving away from it.

_____

b. Write an expression for the distance between the second car and the landmark in terms of the number of hours spent driving t if the car is driving away from it.

_____

c. Use your answers to parts a and b to write an expression for the distance between the two cars in terms of the number of hours spent driving t if the cars are on the same side of the landmark and driving in the same direction away from the landmark. Show your work.

_____

_____

_____

d. Use your answers to parts a and b to write an expression for the distance between the two cars in terms of the number of hours spent driving t if the cars are on opposite sides of the landmark and driving in opposite directions away from the landmark. Show your work.

_____

_____

_____

Name _____ Date _____ Class_____

The student will find zeros of polynomials using suitable factorizations, and use the zeros to draw the graph.

SELECTED RESPONSE
Select the correct answer.

1. Which of the following polynomial functions could have the graph shown?

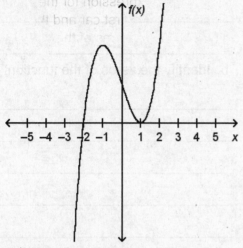

   Ⓐ $f(x) = (x - 2)(x + 1)$

   Ⓑ $f(x) = (x - 2)(x + 1)(x + 1)$

   Ⓒ $f(x) = (x + 2)(x - 1)$

   Ⓓ $f(x) = (x + 2)(x - 1)(x - 1)$

2. Use the numbers below to complete the statement.

   The graph of $f(x) = (x - 6)(x^2 - 3x - 18)$ passes through the x-axis [ ] time(s)

   and is tangent to the x-axis [ ] time(s).

   | 0 | | 1 | | 2 | | 3 | | 4 |

Select all correct answers.

3. Which of the following polynomial functions have graphs that intersect the horizontal axis at least twice?

   Ⓐ $f(x) = x^2 + 10x + 9$

   Ⓑ $f(x) = x^2 - 10x + 25$

   Ⓒ $f(x) = x^2 - 81$

   Ⓓ $f(x) = (x - 1)(x^2 + 9x + 20)$

   Ⓔ $f(x) = (x - 4)(x^2 - 8x + 16)$

   Ⓕ $f(x) = (x + 2)(x^2 - 4x + 4)$

CONSTRUCTED RESPONSE

4. Let $f(x) = -(x + 3)(x - 4)$.

   a. Identify the zeros of the function.

   _____

   _____

   _____

   _____

   _____

   b. Sketch a graph of the function.

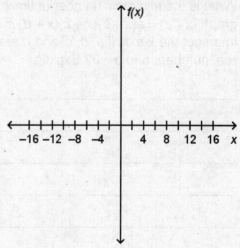

5. Let $g(t) = (t + 2)(t^2 - 5t + 4)$.

   a. Identify the zeros of the function. Show your work.

   _____

   _____

   _____

   _____

   _____

   _____

   b. Sketch a graph of the function.

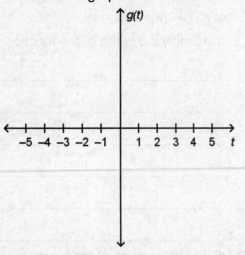

6. What is the minimum number of times the graph of $f(x) = a(x + b)(x + c)(x + d)$ must intersect the x-axis if $a, b, c,$ and d are real numbers and $a \neq 0$? Explain.

   _____

   _____

   _____

   _____

   _____

   _____

7. The width of a rectangular prism is three units longer than its length and four units shorter than its height.

   a. Write a polynomial function for the volume of the rectangular prism $V(w)$ in terms of the width of the rectangular prism w.

   _____

   _____

   b. Identify the zeros of the function.

   _____

   _____

   _____

   _____

   _____

   _____

   c. Sketch a graph of the function.

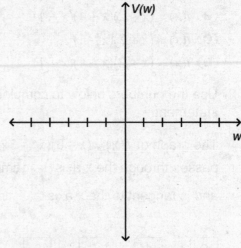

   d. Which part of the graph could not represent a real prism? Explain.

   _____

   _____

   _____

   _____

   _____

   _____

   _____

Name _____ Date _____ Class_____

The student will create equations and inequalities in one variable and use them to solve problems.

SELECTED RESPONSE
Select the correct answer.

1. A landscaper is planting a row of 10 shrubs along the walkway shown below. There must be one shrub at the very beginning and one shrub at the very end, and the shrubs in between will be equally spaced along the length of the walkway. Which equation can the landscaper use to find the distance d in feet to leave between the shrubs?

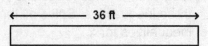
← 36 ft →

Ⓐ $36d = 10$

Ⓑ $9d = 36$

Ⓒ $10d = 36$

Ⓓ $36d = 9$

2. National Cell charges a $5 flat fee for a text messaging plan and $0.15 per text. World Wireless doesn't charge a flat fee, but it charges $0.19 per text. Which inequality and solution represent the number t of texts for which World Wireless is cheaper than National Cell?

Ⓐ $19t > 15t + 5; t > 1.25$

Ⓑ $0.19t > 0.15t + 5; t > 125$

Ⓒ $19t < 15t + 5; t < 1.25$

Ⓓ $0.19t < 0.15t + 5; t < 125$

3. Jennifer, Luis, Robert, Anna, and Tonya are figuring out how to split the check for lunch. The total bill is $65.45. Anna puts in $15, and Tonya puts in $8. The rest of the group splits the rest of the bill equally. Which equation and solution represent the amount a that each of the remaining people pay?

Ⓐ $3a + 23 = 65.45; a = \$14.15$

Ⓑ $5a = 65.45 + 15 + 8; a = \$17.69$

Ⓒ $3a = 88.45; a = \$29.49$

Ⓓ $5a + 23 = 65.45; a = \$8.49$

4. Asako deposits $1000 into a bank account that pays 1.5% interest compounded annually. Which inequality can she use to determine the minimum time in years t she needs to wait before the value of the account is 20% more than its original value?

Ⓐ $1000 \cdot 1.015t > 1200$

Ⓑ $1000 \cdot 1.015t > 1.2$

Ⓒ $1.015^t > 1200$

Ⓓ $1.015^t > 1.2$

5. Which inequality and solution represent keeping the area of a triangle under 36 square feet if the height is twice the length of the base b?

Ⓐ $2b < 36; b < 18$

Ⓑ $\frac{1}{2}b^2 < 36; b < 6\sqrt{2}$

Ⓒ $b^2 < 36; b < 6$

Ⓓ $2b^2 < 36; b < 3\sqrt{2}$

Select all correct answers.

6. A department store offers a frequent-buyers reward card. Every time a customer earns 100 or more points, the customer receives a gift certificate. Each purchase is worth 12 points, and customers automatically earn 25 points when they sign up. Circle the inequalities that could be solved to find the number p of purchases that a customer needs to make in order to earn the first gift certificate.

$12p + 25 < 100$	$12p + 25 > 100$
$12p + 25 \geq 100$	$12p - 25 \geq 100$
$12p - 25 \leq 100$	$12p + 25 \leq 100$
$25 \geq 100 - 12p$	$25 \leq 100 - 12p$
$25 < 100 - 12p$	$12p \geq 100 - 25$

Name _____ Date _____ Class _____

Select the correct answer for each lettered part

7. While rock climbing, Farrell starts at 10 feet above sea level and climbs upward at a rate of 3 feet per minute. Theresa starts at 250 feet above sea level and climbs down at a rate of 2.5 feet per minute. Tell whether each equation can be used to find the time t in minutes it takes for the two climbers to reach the same height.

   a. $10 + 3t = 250 - 2.5t$ ○ Yes ○ No

   b. $10 + 3t = 250 + 2.5t$ ○ Yes ○ No

   c. $3t + 2.5t = 240$ ○ Yes ○ No

   d. $3t = 2.5t$ ○ Yes ○ No

CONSTRUCTED RESPONSE

8. A computer user is downloading a document that is 58 megabytes. The download speed is 0.7 megabytes per second, and 25% of the file has been downloaded. Write and solve an equation to find how many seconds are left before the download is complete. Round your answer to the nearest second.

   _____

   _____

9. A grocery store offers a coupon for $2 off when a customer buys 6 or more bottles of water. The water costs $1.75 per bottle. Shauna uses the function $t(b) = 1.75b - 2$ to find the total t dollars it costs to buy b bottles of water. When she uses the function to find how many bottles she can buy for $5, she finds $b = 4$, so she concludes she could buy 4 bottles of water for $5. Explain what error Shauna made.

   _____

   _____

   _____

10. The length of any side of a triangle is less than the sum of the lengths of the other two sides of the triangle. If three side lengths do not satisfy this requirement, then a triangle cannot be formed from them.

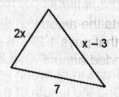

   a. Given the triangle above, use the restriction on side lengths to write three inequalities. Solve all three inequalities for x.

   _____

   _____

   _____

   _____

   _____

   _____

   b. What values of x will satisfy the inequalities you found in part a? Explain how you know.

   _____

   _____

   _____

   _____

   _____

   _____

   c. Give an example of one set of possible side lengths for the triangle above.

   _____

   _____

The student will create equations for relationships between quantities and graph equations on coordinate axes.

SELECTED RESPONSE
Select the correct answer.

1. Which of the following equations represents the amount A in a bank account that pays 1.2% interest compounded annually t years after $2000 is deposited into the account?

   Ⓐ $A = 2000 + 1.2t$

   Ⓑ $A = 2000 + 1.012t$

   Ⓒ $A = 2000(1.2)^t$

   Ⓓ $A = 2000(1.012)^t$

2. Circle the equation that makes a true statement.

   Rita reads a book at a steady pace. Rita graphs her progress through the book by putting the time in hours t on the horizontal axis and chapters remaining C on the vertical axis.

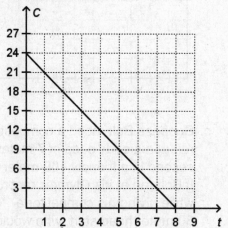

   An equation that describes Rita's graph

   is
   $$C = -3t + 24$$
   $$C = 3t - 24$$
   $$C = -24t + 3$$
   $$C = 24t + 3$$

CONSTRUCTED RESPONSE

3. John is taking part in a charity run. He has received $250 in fixed pledges, and he will receive $25 more in pledges for each mile he runs. Write an equation for the amount of money P John will earn in terms of the distance d he runs, measured in miles.

   _____

   _____

   _____

4. The radioactive element Polonium-210 has a half-life of about 138 days. This means that approximately 0.5% of a mass of Polonium-210 will decay every day. Write an equation for the approximate remaining mass m of 50 grams of Polonium-210 after t days.

   _____

   _____

   _____

5. Julius is flying home to Los Angeles from Boston. His distance away from home in miles d can be expressed in terms of t hours by the equation $d = 2600 - 500t$. Graph Julius's distance away from home in miles d after t hours, choosing appropriate scales.

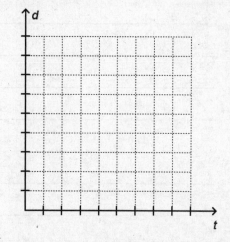

6. The height above the ground in feet of an object h with an initial upward velocity in feet per second v_0 and an initial height in feet h_0 is $h = -16t^2 + v_0 t + h_0$, where t is the time in seconds. A baseball player hits a ball 3 feet above the ground with an initial upward velocity of 96 feet per second. Write an equation for the height of the ball above the ground in feet h in terms of time in seconds t, graph the equation, choosing appropriate axis labels and scales, and then determine the maximum height of the ball. Show your work.

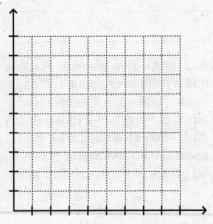

_____
_____
_____
_____
_____
_____
_____
_____
_____

7. At the 2012 Summer Olympics in London, Jamaican sprinter Usain Bolt set a new Olympic record by completing the 100-meter dash in 9.63 seconds.

a. Assuming Bolt ran the race at a steady pace, write an equation for the distance in meters d that Bolt ran after t seconds. Round values to two decimal places as needed.

_____
_____

b. Graph the equation in part a, choosing appropriate axis labels and scales.

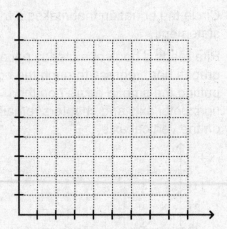

c. Suppose Bolt raced a competitor who ran at a steady pace of 7 meters per second in a friendly 100-meter dash. If Bolt ran at his Olympic record pace while giving his competitor a 30-meter head start, who would win the race? Use a graph to justify your answer. (You can add to the graph in part b or create a new graph on a separate piece of paper.)

_____
_____
_____
_____
_____

The student will represent constraints by equations, inequalities, or systems, and interpret solutions in context.

SELECTED RESPONSE

Select the correct answer.

1. A local supermarket sells chicken for $2.49/lb and pork for $3.19/lb. Todd buys c pounds of chicken and p pounds of pork. Which of the following inequalities represents that Todd only has $40 to spend?

   Ⓐ $2.49c \le 40$

   Ⓑ $3.19p \le 40$

   Ⓒ $c + p \le 40$

   Ⓓ $2.49c + 3.19p \le 40$

2. Sheila is organizing desks in her classroom in preparation for a class of at least 25 students. She wants the desks to be arranged in a rectangle. Due to the dimensions of her classroom, she cannot reasonably fit more than 6 desks in any row or 7 desks in any column. When trying to figure out how Sheila can arrange her room, which of the following is not a meaningful criterion in terms of the number of rows of desks r and the number of columns of desks c?

   Ⓐ $r \le 6$ Ⓒ $r + c \ge 25$

   Ⓑ $c \le 7$ Ⓓ $rc \ge 25$

3. Tucker is planting corn and tomatoes. He has 100 acres of farmland and wants to plant no less than 20 acres of each crop. Indicate by putting a check mark in the appropriate column of the table whether each inequality is a meaningful constraint on whether Tucker can plant c acres of corn and t acres of tomatoes.

	Yes	No
$c \ge 20$		
$t < 20$		
$c + t \ge 100$		
$c + t \le 100$		
$100 - c \ge 80$		

CONSTRUCTED RESPONSE

4. Denise wants to burn at least 5000 calories a week through running. Based on her running speed, she estimates that she can burn 550 calories per hour. Write an inequality that represents Denise's goal in terms of the number of hours spent running h. If Denise runs for one half hour each week day and one hour each weekend day, will she meet her goal? Justify your answer.

   _____

   _____

   _____

   _____

   _____

   _____

   _____

   _____

5. What are the possible dimensions of a 28-square-foot garden if the width is 3 feet shorter than the length? Show your work and explain whether or not the solutions to the equation you write are reasonable answers to the question.

   _____

   _____

   _____

   _____

   _____

   _____

   _____

   _____

6. Carmen and her family visit a restaurant with $45 on hand. The meal tax in the area is 5%. The family also expects to give an 18% tip.

   a. Write an inequality representing the amount of money Carmen's family can spend on dinner in terms of the cost of their meal C if they only spend their on-hand cash.

   _____

   b. Could the family order three $8.49 hamburgers, three $2.49 drinks, and one $4.99 appetizer and pay using only their on-hand cash? Justify your answer.

   _____
   _____
   _____
   _____
   _____

7. John is participating in a charity run. He has gathered $485 in fixed donations and will earn an additional $65 for every mile he runs.

   a. Write an equation for the total amount of money A John will raise for running d miles.

   _____

   b. Rewrite the equation in part a as an inequality that represents that John wants to raise at least $1000.

   _____
   _____

   c. How far does John need to run to meet his goal? Show your work. Assume John only receives donations for completed miles.

   _____

8. Ito has $225, and he wants to expand his media collection by adding some CDs and DVDs.

   a. Ito would like to buy three more CDs than DVDs. Write an equation to represent this condition.

   _____

   b. The store charges $15 for a CD and $25 for a DVD. Write an inequality to represent the constraint on total cost, and then use part a to find the maximum number of DVDs Ito can buy.

   _____
   _____
   _____
   _____
   _____

   c. If Ito purchases the number of DVDs you found in part b and the number of CDs described by part a, how much money will he have left over? Show your work.

   _____
   _____
   _____
   _____
   _____
   _____
   _____
   _____

The student will rearrange formulas to highlight a given quantity, using the same reasoning as in solving equations.

SELECTED RESPONSE
Select the correct answer.

1. Which of the following operations will solve Ohm's law, $V = IR$, for I?

   Ⓐ Subtract R from both sides.

   Ⓑ Divide both sides by R.

   Ⓒ Subtract V from both sides.

   Ⓓ Divide both sides by I.

Select all correct answers.

2. The ideal gas law, $PV = nRT$, is a well-known equation in science that describes the behavior of gases. P is the pressure of the gas, V is the volume of the gas, n is the amount of the gas, R is a constant, and T is the temperature of the gas. Which of the following statements about the ideal gas law are true?

   Ⓐ Dividing both sides of the equation by V results in an equation solved for P.

   Ⓑ Dividing both sides of the equation by R results in an equation solved for T.

   Ⓒ Subtracting P from both sides of the equation results in an equation solved for V.

   Ⓓ Dividing both sides of the equation by RT results in an equation solved for n.

   Ⓔ Subtracting PV from both sides of the equation and then dividing both sides of the equation by $nT - PV$ results in an equation solved for R.

Match each task with the resulting formula.

The surface area A of a rectangular prism with a given length L, width W, and height H is $A = 2LW + 2LH + 2WH$. Write the correct formula from the list below.

3. Solving for the length of a rectangular prism with a given width, height, and surface area

4. Solving for the width of a rectangular prism with a given length, height, and surface area

5. Solving for the height of a rectangular prism with a given length, width, and surface area

$$W = \frac{A}{2H + 2L} - \frac{LH}{H + L}$$

$$L = \frac{HW - 0.5A}{W - H}$$

$$H = \frac{0.5A - LW}{L + W}$$

$$W = \frac{LH - 0.5A}{H - L}$$

$$H = \frac{A + 2LW}{2(L + W)}$$

$$L = \frac{-WH + \frac{1}{2}A}{H + W}$$

CONSTRUCTED RESPONSE

6. The formula for passing efficiency P in NCAA football is

$$P = \frac{8.4Y + 330T + 100C - 200I}{A}$$

where Y is the number of passing yards, T is the number of passing touchdowns, C is the number of completed passes, I is the number of interceptions, and A is the number of attempts. Write an equation that will calculate the completed passes for a quarterback with a given passing efficiency, number of passing yards, number of passing touchdowns, number of interceptions, and number of attempts. Show your work.

_____

_____

_____

_____

_____

7. A high school race track is composed of a rectangle and two semicircles.

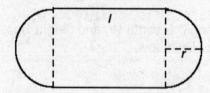

a. If the length l of the rectangle is twice as long as the diameter of the semicircles, write a formula for P, the distance around the track, in terms of the radius r of the semicircles.

_____

b. Rewrite the formula from part a so the radius of the semicircles is given in terms of the distance around the track. Show your work.

_____

_____

8. The formula $D = \sqrt{(x_2 - x_1)^2 + (y_2 - y_1)^2}$ gives the distance between the points (x_1, y_1) and (x_2, y_2) on the coordinate plane.

a. Solve the distance formula for y_2. Show your work.

_____

_____

_____

_____

_____

_____

_____

_____

_____

b. A line with a positive slope passes through the points $(-5, -3)$ and $(1, y)$. If the distance between the two points is 10 units, what is the value of y? How did you decide which of the two values the equation gives is correct? Show your work.

_____

_____

_____

_____

_____

_____

_____

_____

_____

The student will explain each step in solving an equation and construct an argument to justify a solution method.

SELECTED RESPONSE

Select the correct answer.

1. What two properties are used in the following solution to $4b - 3 = 17$?

$$4b - 3 = 17$$
$$4b - 3 + 3 = 17 + 3$$
$$4b = 20$$
$$\frac{4b}{4} = \frac{20}{4}$$
$$b = 5$$

  (A) Addition Property of Equality and Division Property of Equality

  (B) Subtraction Property of Equality and Addition Property of Equality

  (C) Multiplication Property of Equality and Distributive Property

  (D) Subtraction Property of Equality and Zero Product Property

2. Which of the following properties would not be used to justify any of the steps below?

$$\frac{7}{2}n = 3n + 4$$
$$2\left(\frac{7}{2}n\right) = 2(3n + 4)$$
$$7n = 6n + 8$$
$$7n - 6n = 6n + 8 - 6n$$
$$n = 8$$

  (A) Subtraction Property of Equality

  (B) Multiplication Property of Equality

  (C) Distributive Property

  (D) Zero Product Property

Select all correct answers.

3. Examine the solution below.

$$x^2 - 2(2x + 9) = 2x - 2$$
$$x^2 - 4x - 18 = 2x - 2$$
$$x^2 - 4x - 18 + 2 = 2x - 2 + 2$$
$$x^2 - 4x - 16 = 2x$$
$$x^2 - 4x - 16 - 2x = 2x - 2x$$
$$x^2 - 6x - 16 = 0$$
$$(x - 8)(x + 2) = 0$$
$$x - 8 = 0 \text{ or } x + 2 = 0$$
$$x - 8 + 8 = 0 + 8 \text{ or } x + 2 - 2 = 0 - 2$$
$$x = 8 \qquad\qquad x = -2$$

Circle each property below that is used in the solution.

  Addition Property of Equality

  Subtraction Property of Equality

  Multiplication Property of Equality

  Division Property of Equality

  Distributive Property

  Zero Product Property

CONSTRUCTED RESPONSE

4. Examine the given solution process and identify the property that justifies each lettered step.

$$2\left(\frac{1}{2}x + 4x - 7\right) = 2(2x + 3)$$

  a. $x + 8x - 14 = 4x + 6$

     $x + 8x = 4x + 20$

  b. $x + 8x - 4x = 4x + 20 - 4x$

     $5x = 20$

  c. $\frac{5x}{5} = \frac{20}{5}$

     $x = 4$

_____

_____

_____

5. Dennis is driving down the East Coast of the United States. He starts in Boston, Massachusetts, and drives through Hartford, Connecticut, which is approximately 101 miles away from Boston. He continues on from Hartford to Baltimore, Maryland.

    a. Write an equation for the length of Dennis's trip in miles D in terms of the time in hours t it takes him to drive from Hartford to Baltimore and the speed he drives in miles per hour s while traveling from Hartford to Baltimore.

    _____

    b. Baltimore is approximately 410 miles away from Boston. Determine Dennis's average speed from Hartford to Baltimore if that portion of his trip takes 5 hours. Show your work. Justify each step. (You do not need to include "Simplify" as a justification.)

    _____

    _____

    _____

    _____

    _____

    _____

    _____

6. Martina is standing on the edge of a small cliff with the ocean 70 feet below. She throws a small rock out into the ocean with an initial vertical velocity of 32 feet per second. The height in feet h of the rock above the water level after t seconds is modeled by the equation $h = -16t^2 + 32t + 70$. Use the equation to determine how long it takes before the rock is 22 feet above the water. Show your work. Justify each step. (You do not need to include "Simplify" and "Factor" as justifications.)

_____

_____

_____

_____

_____

_____

_____

_____

_____

_____

_____

Name _____ Date _____ Class_____

The student will solve linear equations and inequalities, including equations with coefficients represented by letters.

SELECTED RESPONSE
Select the correct answer.

1. Let a, b, and c be constants, and let x be a variable. Which of the following is equivalent to $a(x + b) < c$ when $a < 0$?

    (A) $x < \dfrac{c - b}{a}$

    (B) $x > \dfrac{c - b}{a}$

    (C) $x < \dfrac{c}{a} - b$

    (D) $x > \dfrac{c}{a} - b$

2. If the perimeter of the pentagon is 35, which of the following is the value of x?

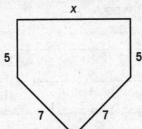

x

5   5

7   7

    (A) 8
    (B) 9
    (C) 10
    (D) 11

Select all correct answers.

3. Which of the following inequalities have solution sets that only include positive numbers?

    (A) $3g - 7 < -2g + 3$
    (B) $-5h + 1 < -2h - 17$
    (C) $8 < -2k + 12$
    (D) $7m + 15 < 8m + 12$
    (E) $2n + 7 - 6n < -10n - 11 + 3n$

4. Ernesto and his family have just finished dinner at a restaurant in a region where the meal tax is 5% of the price of the meal. Ernesto leaves a 17% tip. With tax and tip, the total cost is $58.56. The equation $58.56 = 0.05p + 0.17p + p$, where p is the price of the meal without tax or tip, can be used to model this situation.

Circle each equation that could be a step in the solution of $58.56 = 0.05p + 0.17p + p$ to find the price p of the meal.

$23p = 58.56$ $1.05p = 58.39$

$p = \dfrac{58.56}{1.22}$ $1.22 = \dfrac{p}{58.56}$

$p(1.05 + 0.17) = 58.56$

$p + 0.05p = 58.39$

CONSTRUCTED RESPONSE

5. Solve $-4x + 5 \geq -23$. Show your work.

_____

_____

_____

_____

_____

6. Solve $\dfrac{7\left(-4 - \dfrac{8}{3}x\right)}{-5} = 28$. Show your work.

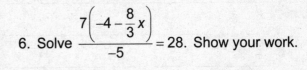

_____

_____

_____

_____

_____

7. Gwendolyn has already read 130 pages of her 400-page summer reading book. If she reads at an average rate of 45 pages per hour, how long will she need to finish the book? Write and solve an equation to find the answer. Show your work.

_____

_____

_____

_____

_____

8. Annika is selling art prints at a comic convention. The convention charged her $50 for her table space, and she is selling her prints at $2 each. Write an equation to represent the net profit P Annika makes from selling a prints, and then determine how many prints she needs to sell if she wants to make $130. How many prints will she need to sell per day if the convention runs from Friday to Sunday? Show your work.

_____

_____

_____

_____

_____

_____

_____

9. A competitor in a 2009 hot dog eating contest set a world record for number of hot dogs and buns eaten in 10 minutes. Let H be the number of hot dogs and buns eaten for the record. Suppose another competitor eats 16 hot dogs in the first 2 minutes of an attempt to at least tie that record. Let r be the average number of hot dogs and buns this competitor must eat per minute in the remaining time.

   a. Write an inequality to represent this situation.

   _____

   b. The record the first competitor set in 2009 was 68 hot dogs and buns. How many hot dogs and buns would the second competitor have to eat per minute over his remaining time to at least tie that record? Show your work.

   _____

   _____

   _____

   _____

   c. If the second competitor maintained his current pace for the entire 10 minutes, would he tie, break, or fall short of the record? Explain.

   _____

   _____

   _____

   _____

   _____

The student will use completing the square to rewrite a quadratic equation and will derive the quadratic formula.

SELECTED RESPONSE
Select the correct answer.

1. Which equation shows $x^2 + 8x + 9 = 0$ after the method of completing the square has been applied?

   (A) $(x + 2)^2 = -5$

   (B) $(x + 4)^2 = 7$

   (C) $(x + 8)^2 = 55$

   (D) $x^2 = -(8x + 9)$

2. Circle the value that makes a true statement.

   When $2x^2 - 20x + 49 = 19$ is written in the form $(x - p)^2 = q$, the

   value of q is
19
10
5
-30
   .

Select all correct answers.

3. Which of the following equations, when rewritten in the form $(x - p)^2 = q$, have a value of q that is a perfect square?

   (A) $x^2 - 2x + 5 = 13$

   (B) $x^2 + 8x + 9 = 5$

   (C) $2x^2 + 12x - 29 = 81$

   (D) $5x^2 - 20x + 14 = -6$

   (E) $3x^2 + 36x + 88 = 4$

Select the correct answer for each lettered part.

4. Determine whether each given equation has equal values of p and q when written in the form $(x - p)^2 = q$.

   a. $x^2 + 6x + 4 = 0$ ○ Yes ○ No

   b. $x^2 - 8x + 1 = -11$ ○ Yes ○ No

   c. $2x^2 + 12x + 37 = 13$ ○ Yes ○ No

   d. $3x^2 - 42x + 127 = 1$ ○ Yes ○ No

   e. $2x^2 + 8x - 5 = -9$ ○ Yes ○ No

CONSTRUCTED RESPONSE

5. Rewrite $x^2 + 14x + 13 = 0$ in the form $(x - p)^2 = q$ by completing the square. Show your work.

_____

_____

_____

6. Rewrite $4x^2 - 16x - 21 = 12$ in the form $(x - p)^2 = q$ by completing the square. Show your work.

_____

_____

_____

7. How many real solutions does $3x^2 + 18x + 77 = 2$ have? Justify your answer by rewriting the equation in the form $(x - p)^2 = q$.

_____

_____

_____

_____

_____

_____

_____

_____

_____

8. Derive the quadratic formula from $ax^2 + bx + c = 0$ by completing the square.

_____

_____

_____

_____

_____

_____

_____

_____

_____

9. A catapult set atop a hill overlooking an enemy castle fires a boulder at that castle. The equation that represents the height h in feet of the boulder above the ground the castle is built on is $h = -16t^2 + 64t + 217$, where t is the time in seconds after the boulder is launched.

a. Rewrite the equation in the form $(x - p)^2 = q$ for the case where a boulder strikes the castle wall 25 feet above the ground. Show your work.

_____

_____

_____

_____

_____

b. How long is the boulder in part a in the air? Show your work.

_____

_____

_____

_____

c. If the boulder has an initial horizontal velocity of 95 feet per second, how far away from the castle wall is the catapult? Show your work.

_____

_____

_____

_____

_____

_____

The student will solve quadratic equations by various methods and will recognize and write complex solutions.

SELECTED RESPONSE
Select the correct answer.

1. Which of the following quadratic equations has no real solutions?

   Ⓐ $3x^2 + 12x + 12 = 0$

   Ⓑ $3x^2 - 3x - 18 = 0$

   Ⓒ $3x^2 + 2x + 1 = 0$

   Ⓓ $3x^2 - 3 = 0$

2. When the quadratic formula is applied to $2x^2 + 3x - 4 = 0$, what is the numerator of the simplified answer?

   Ⓐ $3 \pm \sqrt{41}$

   Ⓑ $-3 \pm \sqrt{41}$

   Ⓒ $3 \pm \sqrt{38}$

   Ⓓ $-3 \pm \sqrt{-23}$

Select all correct answers.

3. Which of the following quadratic equations have two distinct, real solutions?

   Ⓐ $x^2 = 36$

   Ⓑ $x^2 - 78 = 0$

   Ⓒ $x^2 - 8x + 16 = 0$

   Ⓓ $3x^2 - 6x = 29$

   Ⓔ $5x^2 - 4x + 3 = 0$

4. Indicate the number of distinct, real solutions for each equation by putting a check mark in the appropriate column of the table.

	Zero	One	Two
$x^2 + 25 = 10x$			
$x^2 + 3x + 9 = 5$			
$x^2 + x = 72$			
$3x^2 + 36x + 121 = 13$			
$2x^2 - 16 = -7x - 1$			

CONSTRUCTED RESPONSE

5. Solve the quadratic equation $x^2 - 11x + 24 = 0$ by factoring. Show your work.

   _____

   _____

6. Solve the quadratic equation $x^2 - 22x = -57$ by any method. Show your work.

   _____

   _____

7. For what values of b does the equation $5x^2 + bx + 12 = 0$ have no real solutions? Justify your answer.

   _____

   _____

8. A batter makes contact with a baseball 3 feet above the plate and the ball flies with a vertical velocity of 96 feet per second. It eventually lands in outfield bleacher seats 25 feet above the ground. This is modeled by the equation $25 - 3 = -16t^2 + 96t$.

a. Determine the flight time of the ball by completing the square. Round to two decimal places as needed. Explain why you chose the answer you did.

_____

_____

_____

_____

_____

_____

b. If the horizontal velocity of the baseball from part b is 80 feet per second, how far away from the batter does the ball land? Round to the nearest whole foot.

_____

_____

_____

_____

_____

_____

_____

9. A rectangular box has a surface area of 670 square inches. The width is 3 inches greater than the height, and the length is 3 inches less than twice the height. Solve the resulting quadratic equation and then find the three dimensions and the volume of the box. Show your work.

_____

_____

_____

_____

_____

_____

_____

_____

_____

_____

_____

_____

_____

_____

_____

_____

_____

_____

The student will use the sum of one equation and a multiple of another to produce a system with the same solutions.

SELECTED RESPONSE
Select the correct answer.

1. Which of the following systems of equations has the same solution as the given system?

$$\begin{cases} -2x + 2y = -2 \\ 3x - y = 9 \end{cases}$$

Ⓐ $\begin{cases} 4x = 16 \\ 3x - y = 9 \end{cases}$

Ⓑ $\begin{cases} -2x + 2y = -2 \\ 6x - 2y = 9 \end{cases}$

Ⓒ $\begin{cases} -3x - 7y = 3 \\ 3x - y = 9 \end{cases}$

Ⓓ $\begin{cases} -2x + 2y = -2 \\ x + y = 11 \end{cases}$

Select all correct answers.

2. The solution to the system of equations $x + y = 1$ and $x - y = -7$ is $(-3, 4)$. Circle each equation below for which $(-3, 4)$ is NOT a solution.

$x + y - 2(x - y) = 1 - 2(-7)$

$3(x + y) + x - y = 3(1) - 7$

$x + y + 5(x - y) = 5(1) - 7$

$-4(x + y) + x - y = 1 - 4(-7)$

$x + y - x + y = 1 + 7$

CONSTRUCTED RESPONSE

3. Write an equation that is the sum of the first equation and three times the second equation. Combine all like terms on both sides of the equation.

$$\begin{cases} 2x - 3y = 7 \\ 4x + y = -7 \end{cases}$$

_____

_____

_____

4. The solution to the system of equations $2x + y = 5$ and $x + 3y = -5$ is $(4, -3)$.

   a. Write an equation that is the sum of $2x + y = 5$ and -2 times $x + 3y = -5$. Combine all like terms on both sides of the equation.

   _____

   _____

   _____

   b. Without solving, how do you know that the system of equations consisting of $x + 3y = -5$ and your answer from part a has the same solution as the original system?

   _____

   _____

   _____

5. The solution to the following system of equations is $(5, -2)$.

$$\begin{cases} 2x + 3y = 4 \\ x + y = 3 \end{cases}$$

   a. Find the sum of the first equation and twice the second equation. Combine all like terms on both sides of the equation

   _____

   _____

   _____

   b. Verify that the given solution is a solution to your equation from part a.

   _____

   _____

   _____

6. For variables x and y and constants P, Q, R, S, T, U, and v, prove that the solution (x_0, y_0) to the system of equations

$$\begin{cases} Px + Qy = R \\ Sx + Ty = U \end{cases}$$

is also a solution to the system of equations shown below.

$$\begin{cases} Px + Qy = R \\ (P + vS)x + (Q + vT)y = R + vU \end{cases}$$

_____

_____

_____

_____

_____

_____

7. The solution to the system of equations

$$\begin{cases} 3x + 2y = 5 \\ 2x - 3y = 12 \end{cases}$$

is (3, −2). Find the difference between four times the first equation and three times the second equation. Show your work. Then show that (3, −2) is a solution to the system of equations composed of the first original equation and this new equation.

_____

_____

_____

_____

_____

_____

_____

8. The solution to the following system of equations is (−2, 3).

$$\begin{cases} 4x + 3y = 1 \\ x - y = -5 \end{cases}$$

a. Find a system of equations with the same solution by replacing the first equation with the sum of the first equation and three times the second equation.

_____

_____

_____

_____

b. Find another system of equations with the same solution by replacing the first equation with the sum of the first equation and −4 times the second equation.

_____

_____

_____

_____

_____

c. Show that your answers from parts a and b are equivalent systems. (Hint: Can you transform the system from part a into the system from part b by combining equations?)

_____

_____

_____

_____

_____

The student will solve systems of linear equations in two variables exactly and approximately (e.g., with graphs).

SELECTED RESPONSE
Select the correct answer.

1. In which quadrant is the solution to this system of equations?

$$\begin{cases} 2x + 5y = 1 \\ 3x - 4y = 13 \end{cases}$$

Ⓐ Quadrant I

Ⓑ Quadrant II

Ⓒ Quadrant III

Ⓓ Quadrant IV

Select all correct answers.

2. Which of the following systems of equations has a solution in which the *x*-value is greater than the *y*-value?

Ⓐ $\begin{cases} x + 3y = -1 \\ 5x + 4y = 6 \end{cases}$

Ⓑ $\begin{cases} 3x + 2y = -19 \\ -2x - 3y = 21 \end{cases}$

Ⓒ $\begin{cases} 6x - y = -10 \\ -2x - 2y = -6 \end{cases}$

Ⓓ $\begin{cases} 3x + 5y = 16 \\ 4x - y = 6 \end{cases}$

Ⓔ $\begin{cases} 5x - 2y = 12 \\ -10x + 4y = -20 \end{cases}$

3. For each system of equations, indicate the number of solutions by putting a check mark in the appropriate column of the table.

	Zero	One	Infinitely many
$\begin{cases} 2x - y = 1 \\ x + 5y = 6 \end{cases}$			
$\begin{cases} 2x + 3y = 12 \\ 4x + 6y = 24 \end{cases}$			
$\begin{cases} -x + 4y = -17 \\ 2x - 3y = 6 \end{cases}$			
$\begin{cases} 5x + 8y = 6 \\ -3x - 4y = -4 \end{cases}$			
$\begin{cases} 4x - 6y = 15 \\ -6x + 9y = 12 \end{cases}$			

CONSTRUCTED RESPONSE

4. Solve the given system of equations algebraically. Show your work.

$$\begin{cases} 5x - 2y = 4 \\ 3x - 4y = -6 \end{cases}$$

_____

_____

5. Graph $3x + 2y = 7$ and $2x - 5y = -25$ and use the graph to estimate the solution to the system of equations.

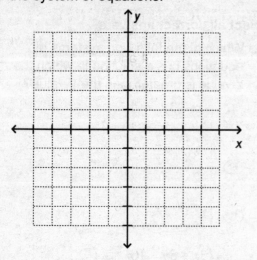

_____

6. Shawntae has 21 coins, all of them nickels and dimes, that are worth $1.70.

   a. Write a system of equations to describe the situation.

_____

   b. Solve the system. Show your work.

_____

_____

_____

_____

_____

_____

   c. How many nickels and how many dimes does Shawntae have?

_____

_____

7. Madeline is selling sketches for $2 and color prints for $5 at a comic convention. Madeline leaves the table and asks her friend Chris to run the table for her. She returns to find Chris has made $93. Chris doesn't know how many of each item he sold, but he remembers that he sold a total of 30 sketches and colored prints. Below is Madeline's work in determining how many of each item was sold.

s = number of sketches
p = number of colored prints
$$s + p = 30$$
$$s = 30 - p$$

$$2s + 5p = 93$$
$$2(30 - p) + 5p = 93$$
$$60 - p + 5p = 93$$
$$60 + 4p = 93$$
$$4p = 33$$
$$p = 8.25$$

   a. As Madeline was writing "$p = 8.25$," she realized she had made a mistake. How did she know?

_____

_____

   b. Explain Madeline's mistake.

_____

_____

_____

   c. How many of each item did Chris sell? Show your work.

_____

_____

_____

_____

_____

_____

Name _____ Date _____ Class_____

The student will solve a linear-quadratic system in two variables algebraically and graphically.

SELECTED RESPONSE

Select the correct answer.

1. What is the distance between the points of intersection of the graphs of $y = x^2$ and $y = 6 - x$?

   Ⓐ $\sqrt{26}$

   Ⓑ $5\sqrt{2}$

   Ⓒ $2\sqrt{37}$

   Ⓓ $\sqrt{170}$

2. How many times do the graphs of $y = -x^2 + 5x + 6$ and $2x + y = 16$ intersect?

   Ⓐ 0

   Ⓑ 1

   Ⓒ 2

   Ⓓ 3

Select all correct answers.

3. Which of the following systems of equations have at least one solution in Quadrant I?

   Ⓐ $\begin{cases} -4x + 3y = 1 \\ y = x^2 - x + 1 \end{cases}$

   Ⓑ $\begin{cases} x - 3y = 2 \\ y = x^2 + 2x - 34 \end{cases}$

   Ⓒ $\begin{cases} 3x + y = -2 \\ y = x^2 - 2x - 4 \end{cases}$

   Ⓓ $\begin{cases} 2x + y = -1 \\ y = -x^2 - 6x - 5 \end{cases}$

   Ⓔ $\begin{cases} x + y = 3 \\ y = x^2 - 8x + 16 \end{cases}$

CONSTRUCTED RESPONSE

4. Find all the points of intersection between the line $2x + y = 4$ and the ellipse $\dfrac{x^2}{4} + \dfrac{y^2}{16} = 1$. Show your work.

   _____

   _____

   _____

   _____

   _____

   _____

   _____

   _____

   _____

   _____

   _____

5. Graph the following system of equations and then solve the system graphically.

   $\begin{cases} 2x + y = -12 \\ y = x^2 - 5 \end{cases}$

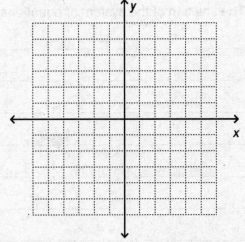

   _____

6. Graph the following system of equations and then solve the system graphically.

$$\begin{cases} -5x + y = 5 \\ x - y^2 = -1 \end{cases}$$

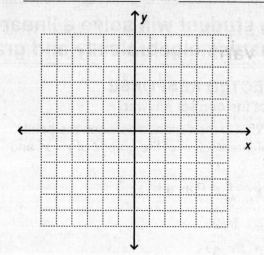

7. Terrell was asked to find the solution(s) of the system of equations $\begin{cases} y = -2x - 5 \\ y = x^2 + 4x - 21 \end{cases}$.

His work and graph are shown. Once Terrell graphed the system of equations to check his answer, he knew he had made a mistake somewhere. State how Terrell knew he made a mistake, identify the mistake, and find the correct solution(s) of the system of equations. Show your work.

$x^2 + 4x - 21 = -2x - 5$

$x^2 + 6x - 16 = 0$

$x = \dfrac{-6 + \sqrt{36 - 4(1)(-16)}}{2}$

$\quad = \dfrac{-6 + \sqrt{100}}{2}$

$\quad = \dfrac{-6 + 10}{2}$

$\quad = 2$

$y = -2(2) - 5 = -9$

The solution of the system of equations is (2, –9).

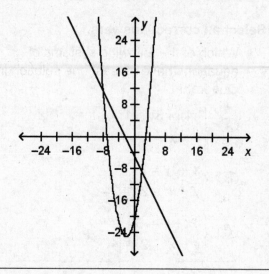

Name _____ Date _____ Class _____

The student will understand that the graph of an equation in two variables is its solutions plotted in the coordinate plane.

SELECTED RESPONSE

1. Circle the correct answer.

   The number of equations graphed below

   that have *P* as a solution is

0
1
2
3

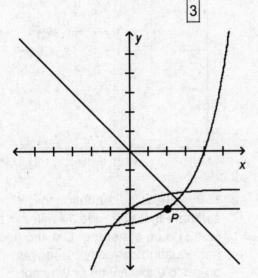

Select the correct answer.

2. Which of the following is NOT a solution of the equation represented by the graph?

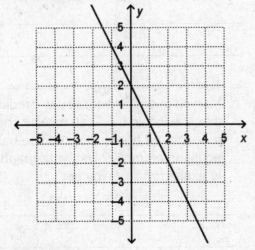

Ⓐ (0, 2)

Ⓑ (1, 0)

Ⓒ (3, –4)

Ⓓ (4, –1)

Select all correct answers.

3. Which of the following are solutions of the equation represented by the graph?

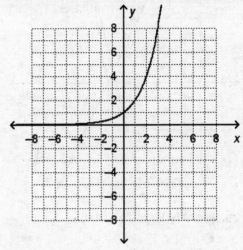

Ⓐ (–4, 1)   Ⓓ (1, 0)

Ⓑ (–1, 2)   Ⓔ (2, 4)

Ⓒ (0, 1)   Ⓕ (3, 8)

CONSTRUCTED RESPONSE

4. A linear equation has a graph that goes through the points shown below and extends infinitely in both directions. Is (13, 9) a solution of this equation? Justify your answer.

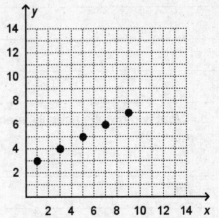

_____

_____

_____

Name _____ Date _____ Class _____

5. Based on the graph, Bryce says that (1, 0) is the solution of $y = 3^x - 3$ and $-4x + y = -2$ because their graphs intersect at that point.

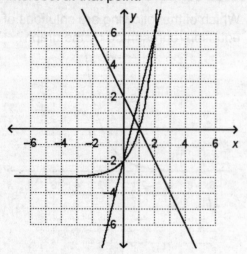

a. Identify Bryce's error.

_____

_____

_____

_____

_____

_____

_____

_____

b. What two graphs actually intersect at (1, 0)?

_____

_____

c. Use the graph to find the solution(s) of $y = 3^x - 3$ and $-4x + y = -2$.

_____

_____

6. Maryse went for a bike ride. She rode at a constant speed, and she traveled 7 miles in one hour. Maryse wrote the equation $y = 7x$ to model her bike ride, where x is the time Maryse spent riding, and y is the distance she traveled.

a. Graph Maryse's equation.

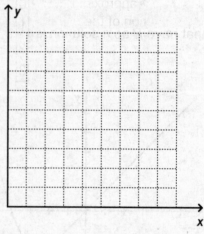

b. Maryse uses her equation to estimate that she rode 14 miles in the first 2 hours of her trip. Did she use her equation correctly? Use your graph to explain why or why not.

_____

_____

_____

_____

c. Maryse uses her equation to predict that she would travel 40 miles if she rode for four hours. Did she use her equation correctly? Use your graph to explain why or why not.

_____

_____

_____

_____

_____

_____

The student will use intersection(s) of the graphs of $f(x)$ and $g(x)$ to approximate solution(s) of the equation $f(x) = g(x)$.

SELECTED RESPONSE

Select the correct answer.

1. Circle the correct answer.

   The best approximate value of x that is the solution of the equation $a(x) = b(x)$

   is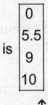

0
5.5
9
10

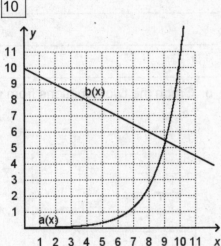

CONSTRUCTED RESPONSE

2. Graph the equations $y = 2^x$ and $y = 4x$. Use the graph to estimate the solution(s) of the equation $2^x = 4x$.

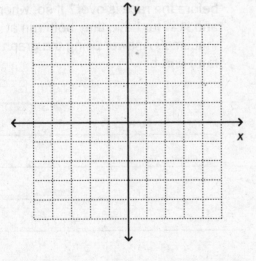

_____

_____

3. a. Complete the table of values below.

x	$4x + 8$	$7x - 11$
5		
5.5		
6		
6.5		
7		
7.5		

   b. Use the table to determine an approximate solution of $4x + 8 = 7x - 11$. Justify why your solution is the best approximation given in the table.

   _____

   _____

   _____

   _____

   _____

   _____

4. Why are the x-coordinates of the points where the graphs of the equations $y = f(x)$ and $y = g(x)$ intersect the solutions of the equation $f(x) = g(x)$?

   _____

   _____

   _____

   _____

   _____

   _____

   _____

   _____

   _____

   _____

   _____

   _____

5. Chris deposits $1200 into a bank account that pays 1.5% interest compounded annually. At the same time, Karla deposits $1250 into a bank account that earns 0.9% interest compounded annually. Neither Chris nor Karla withdraws money from or deposits more money into his or her account.

   a. Write functions $c(t)$ and $k(t)$ that represent the amount of money in Chris's account and the amount of money in Karla's account, respectively, after t years.

_____

_____

_____

   b. Complete the table of values for each account. Round all values to the nearest cent.

Year	Chris's Account	Karla's Account
3		
4		
5		
6		
7		
8		

   c. Which row in the table represents the best approximation of the intersection of the graphs of $c(t)$ and $k(t)$? Explain how you know.

_____

_____

_____

_____

_____

_____

6. The hare has challenged the tortoise to a race. The hare offers the tortoise a 435-meter head start. The race path is 500 meters long, and the tortoise moves at a rate of 5 meters per minute. The hare knows that he moves at a rate 30 times as fast as the tortoise.

   a. Write functions $g(t)$ and $h(t)$ that represent the distance d, in meters, the tortoise and the hare, respectively, have traveled t minutes after the hare begins running.

_____

_____

_____

   b. Graph the two equations from part a.

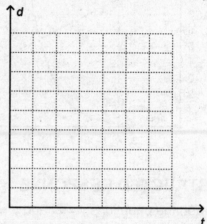

   c. Does the hare pass the tortoise before the race is over? If so, when, and how far have they both run at that time? Answer using the graph from part b.

_____

_____

_____

_____

_____

_____

_____

The student will graph linear inequalities as a half-plane and systems of linear inequalities as intersections of half-planes.

SELECTED RESPONSE
Select the correct answer.

1. Describe the graph that represents the solutions of the inequality $y < 5x + 12$.

   Ⓐ All of the points that lie above the line $y = 5x + 12$

   Ⓑ All of the points that lie on and above the line $y = 5x + 12$

   Ⓒ All of the points that lie below the line $y = 5x + 12$

   Ⓓ All of the points that lie on and below the line $y = 5x + 12$

2. Which of the following systems represents the graph shown?

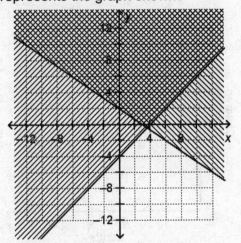

   Ⓐ $\begin{cases} 2x + 3y < 6 \\ -x + y > -4 \end{cases}$

   Ⓑ $\begin{cases} 2x + 3y \geq 6 \\ -x + y \geq -4 \end{cases}$

   Ⓒ $\begin{cases} x + y \geq 4 \\ 2x - 3y \leq 6 \end{cases}$

   Ⓓ $\begin{cases} x + y > 4 \\ 2x - 3y < 6 \end{cases}$

Select all correct answers.

3. Circle each inequality below that has the solutions graphed.

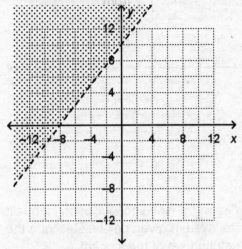

$5x - 4y < -40$

$5x + 4y > 40$

$y \geq \dfrac{5}{4}x + 10$

$y > \dfrac{5}{4}x + 10$

$-10x + 8y \leq 80$

$-10x + 8y > 80$

CONSTRUCTED RESPONSE

4. Graph the solutions of the inequality $3x - 6y \leq 30$.

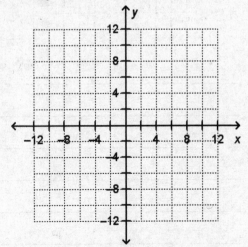

Name _____ Date _____ Class_____

5. Graph the solution set of the system.

$$\begin{cases} 8x + 5y > 40 \\ -6x + 2y \ge -18 \end{cases}$$

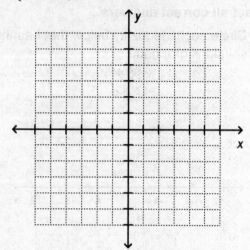

6. Graph the solutions for each inequality in the system given below. Describe the solution set of the system.

$$\begin{cases} 6x + 8y \ge 24 \\ -3x - 4y \ge 18 \end{cases}$$

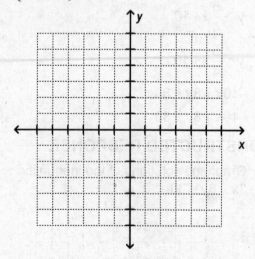

_____

_____

_____

_____

_____

_____

7. A company provides bus trips to various events for a adults and c children. The company charges $15 for each adult and $8 for each child for a trip to an upcoming play. The bus has a maximum capacity of 40 people, and the company needs to earn a minimum of $400 from this event to make a profit.

a. Write a system of inequalities that represents this situation.

_____

_____

_____

_____

b. Graph the system of inequalities from part a.

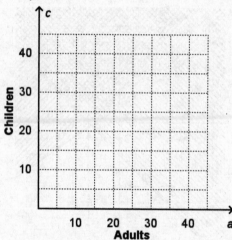

c. 20 adults and 15 children are going to the play. Can the bus hold that many people and does the company make a profit? Explain by using the graph from part b.

_____

_____

_____

_____

_____

_____

Name _____ Date _____ Class _____

The student will understand the definition of a function in terms of domain and range and its corresponding graph.

SELECTED RESPONSE
Select the correct answer.

1. What are the domain and range of the function $y = f(x)$ as shown on the graph?

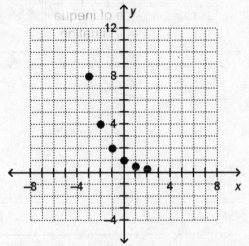

Ⓐ The domain is {0.25, 0.5, 1, 2, 4, 8}, and the range is {−3, −2, −1, 0, 1, 2}.

Ⓑ The domain is {−3, −2, −1, 0, 1, 2} and the range is {0.25, 0.5, 1, 2, 4, 8}.

Ⓒ The domain is all real numbers between −3 and 2, and the range is all real numbers between 0.25 and 8.

Ⓓ The domain is all real numbers between 0.25 and 8, and the range is all real numbers between −3 and 2.

2. The linear function $f(x)$ has the domain $x \geq 5$. Which of the following does not represent an element of the range?

Ⓐ $f\left(2\dfrac{1}{2}\right)$

Ⓑ $f(5)$

Ⓒ $f(10.5868)$

Ⓓ $f(100,000)$

Select all correct answers.

3. The domain of the function $f(x)$ is the set of integers greater than −5. Circle each value that represents an element of the range of f.

$f\left(-\dfrac{14}{5}\right)$ $f\left(\dfrac{1}{2}\right)$ $f\left(\dfrac{18}{3}\right)$

$f(4.8)$ $f(-2)$ $f(-5)$

$f(0)$ $f(-8)$ $f(14)$

CONSTRUCTED RESPONSE

4. Examine the two sets below. The first is the set of months in the year and the second is the possible numbers of days per month. Is the relation that maps the month to its possible number of days a function? Explain.

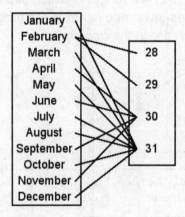

_____

_____

_____

_____

_____

_____

_____

5. Does the table represent a function? If so, state the domain and range. If not, state why.

x	f(x)
−2	2
−1	6
0	10
1	14
2	18

_____

_____

_____

_____

6. The graph of $y = -\dfrac{1}{2}x + 3$ is shown below. Use the graph to find the y-values associated with $x = -2$, $x = 0$, and $x = 2$. If $y = f(x)$ is a function, which of the values given above are in the range and which are in the domain?

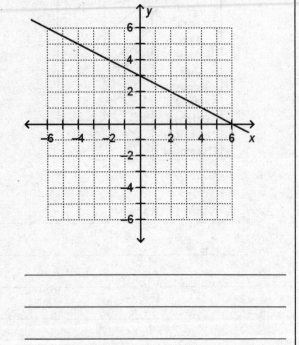

_____

_____

_____

_____

_____

7. An exponential function $y = f(x)$ is graphed below. The graph has a horizontal asymptote at $y = -3$. What are the domain and range of $f(x)$?

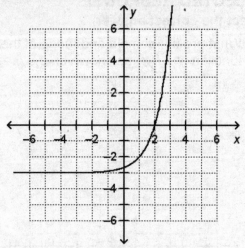

_____

_____

8. Determine whether the following situations represent functions. Explain your reasoning. If the situation represents a function, give the domain and range.

a. Each U.S. coin is mapped to its monetary value.

_____

_____

_____

_____

_____

b. A $1, $5, $10, $20, $50, or $100 bill is mapped to all the sets of coins that are the same total value as the bill.

_____

_____

_____

_____

_____

Name _____ Date _____ Class_____

The student will use function notation, evaluate functions, and interpret statements in terms of a context.

SELECTED RESPONSE
Select the correct answer.

1. What is the value of the function $f(x) = x^2 - 5x + 2$ evaluated at $x = 2$?

   Ⓐ −4

   Ⓑ 2

   Ⓒ 6

   Ⓓ 16

2. Joshua is driving to the store. The average distance d, in miles, he travels over t minutes is given by the function $d(t) = 0.5t$. What is the value of the function when $t = 15$?

   Ⓐ 75 miles

   Ⓑ 7.5 minutes

   Ⓒ 7.5 miles

   Ⓓ 15 minutes

3. Marcello is tiling his kitchen floor with 45 square tiles. The tiles come in whole-number side lengths of 6 to 12 inches. The function $A(s) = 45s^2$, where s is the side length of the tile, represents the area that Marcello can cover with the tiles. What is the domain of this function?

   Ⓐ All real numbers between 6 and 12, inclusive

   Ⓑ All rational numbers between 6 and 12, inclusive

   Ⓒ {6, 7, 8, 9, 10, 11, 12}

   Ⓓ {6, 12}

Select all correct answers.

4. The table shows values in the range of $f(x) = -6x + 11$. Using the values at the right, complete the table by writing the corresponding values in the domain of f.

x	$f(x)$
	−37
	−25
	−13
	−1

1	5
2	6
3	7
4	8

CONSTRUCTED RESPONSE

5. The production cost for g graphing calculators is $C(g) = 25g$. Evaluate the function at $g = 15$. What does the value of the function at $g = 15$ represent?

   _____

   _____

   _____

   _____

   _____

   _____

6. The domain of the function $f(x) = 13x - x^2$ is given as {−2, −1, 0, 1, 2}. What is the range? Show your work.

   _____

   _____

   _____

   _____

   _____

   _____

7. Victor needs to find the volume of cube-shaped containers with side lengths ranging from 2 feet to 7 feet. The side lengths of the containers can only be whole numbers. The volume of a container with side length s is given by $V(s) = s^3$.

   a. What is the domain of the function?

   _____

   _____

   b. Evaluate the function at each value in the domain. Show your work.

   _____

   _____

   _____

   _____

   _____

8. A store selling televisions is calculating the profit for one model. Currently, the store has 25 televisions in stock. The store bought these televisions from a supplier for $99.50 each. Each television will be sold for $149.99.

   a. Write a profit function in terms of n, the number of televisions sold.

   _____

   b. What is the domain of the function? Explain.

   _____

   _____

   _____

   c. If the store sold all of the televisions in stock, how much would the profit be?

   _____

9. Tanya is printing a report. There are 100 sheets of paper in the printer, and the number of sheets p left after t minutes of printing is given by the function $p(t) = -8t + 100$.

   a. How long would it take the printer to use all 100 sheets of paper? Explain how you found your answer.

   _____

   _____

   _____

   _____

   b. What is the domain of the function? Explain.

   _____

   _____

   _____

   _____

   c. What is the range of the function? Explain.

   _____

   _____

   _____

   _____

   d. Tanya's report takes 7 minutes to print. How long is Tanya's report? Show your work.

   _____

   _____

   _____

The student will recognize that sequences are functions whose domain is a subset of the integers.

SELECTED RESPONSE
Select the correct answer.

1. Which function below generates the sequence −2, 0, 2, 4, 6, …?

   Ⓐ $f(n) = n - 2$, where $n \geq 0$ and n is an integer.

   Ⓑ $f(n) = 2n - 2$, where $n \geq 0$ and n is an integer.

   Ⓒ $f(n) = -2n + 2$, where $n \geq 1$ and n is an integer.

   Ⓓ $f(n) = 2n$, where $n \geq 0$ and n is an integer.

2. The sequence −1, 2, 7, 14, … can be generated by the function $f(n) = n^2 - 2$. What is the domain of the function?

   Ⓐ The domain is the set of all positive real numbers.

   Ⓑ The domain is the set of all real numbers greater than 1.

   Ⓒ The domain is the set of integers n such that $n \geq 0$.

   Ⓓ The domain is the set of integers n such that $n \geq 1$.

Select all correct answers.

3. Which of the functions below could be used to generate the sequence 1, 2, 4, 8, 16, 32, …?

   Ⓐ $f(n) = 2^n$, where $n \geq 0$ and n is an integer.

   Ⓑ $f(n) = 2^n$, where $n \geq 1$ and n is an integer.

   Ⓒ $f(1) = 1$, $f(n) = 2(f(n - 1))$, where $n \geq 2$ and n is an integer.

   Ⓓ $f(n) = 2(n - 1)$, where $n \geq 1$ and n is an integer.

   Ⓔ $f(n) = n^2$, where $n \geq 1$ and n is an integer.

Match each sequence with the correct function.

For each sequence, write a function that generates it. Assume that n is an integer.
Select from the functions below.

4. 4, 12, 24, 40, 60, …

5. 0, $\dfrac{1}{2}$, $\dfrac{2}{3}$, $\dfrac{3}{4}$, $\dfrac{4}{5}$, …

6. 48, 24, 12, 6, 3, …

7. 3, 6, 9, 12, 15, …

8. 3, 6, 11, 18, 27, …

$f(n) = 2n(n + 1)$, $n \geq 1$

$f(n) = 2(n + 2)$, $n \geq 0$

$f(n) = \dfrac{n - 1}{n}$, $n \geq 1$

$f(n) = \dfrac{n}{n + 1}$, $n \geq 1$

$f(n) = n^2 + 2$, $n \geq 1$

$f(n) = 3n$, $n \geq 1$

$f(1) = 48$ and $f(n) = \dfrac{1}{2} f(n - 1)$, $n \geq 2$

$f(1) = 48$ and $f(n) = 2f(n - 1)$, $n \geq 2$

CONSTRUCTED RESPONSE

9. Consider the sequence 1, 2, 5, 10, 17, ...

    a. Write a quadratic function $f(n)$ that generates the sequence. Assume that the domain of the function is the set of integers $n \geq 0$.

    _____

    b. Use your result from part a to determine the 15th term of the sequence.

    _____

    _____

    _____

    _____

10. The domain of a function f defining the sequence $\frac{2}{3}, \frac{3}{4}, \frac{4}{5}, \frac{5}{6}, \frac{6}{7}, \ldots$ is the set of consecutive integers starting with 1.

    a. What is $f(3)$? Explain.

    _____

    _____

    _____

    _____

    b. How does your answer to part a change if the domain of the function is the set of consecutive integers starting with 0?

    _____

    _____

    _____

    _____

    _____

11. The Fibonacci sequence is 1, 1, 2, 3, 5, 8, 13, 21, ...

    a. Write a recursive function to describe the terms of the Fibonacci sequence. Begin with the conditions $f(0) = f(1) = 1$ and $f(2) = f(1) + f(0)$.

    _____

    _____

    b. Suppose the first two terms of the Fibonacci sequence were $f(0) = 2$ and $f(1) = 2$, instead of $f(0) = 1$ and $f(1) = 1$. Write the first 5 terms of the sequence.

    _____

    _____

    c. Explain how you can modify your answer from part a to describe the terms of the sequence found in part b.

    _____

    _____

    _____

    _____

    _____

    _____

12. Consider the sequence 1, 3, 5, 7, 9, ...

    a. Write a function describing the sequence whose domain is the set of consecutive integers starting with 1.

    _____

    b. Write a recursive function describing the sequence.

    _____

    _____

    _____

Name _____ Date _____ Class_____

The student will interpret key features of graphs and tables, and sketch graphs showing key features given a description.

SELECTED RESPONSE

Select the correct answer.

1. The graph shows the height $h(t)$ of a model rocket t seconds after it is launched from the ground at 48 feet per second. Where is the height of the rocket increasing? Where is it decreasing?

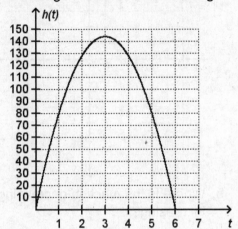

Ⓐ The height of the rocket is always increasing.

Ⓑ The height of the rocket is always decreasing.

Ⓒ The height of the rocket is increasing when $0 < t < 3$ and decreasing when $3 < t < 6$.

Ⓓ The height of the rocket is increasing when $3 < t < 6$ and decreasing when $0 < t < 3$.

Select all correct answers.

2. Circle each statement that is true about the graph.

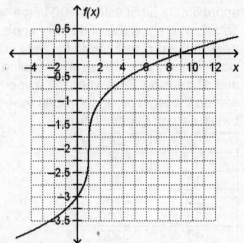

The x-intercept is 9.

The y-intercept is –2.

$f(x)$ is increasing when $x < 1$.

$f(x)$ is decreasing when $x > 1$.

$f(x)$ has a local maximum at $(1, -2)$.

$f(x)$ has a local minimum at $(1, -2)$.

$f(x)$ is negative when $x < 9$.

$f(x)$ is positive when $x > -2$.

CONSTRUCTED RESPONSE

3. Martha's text message plan costs $15.00 for the first 1000 text messages sent plus $0.25 per text over 1000 sent. Let $C(t)$ represent the cost of sending t text messages over 1000. Sketch a graph of this relationship, and find and interpret the $C(t)$-intercept.

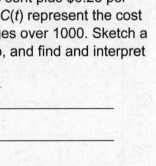

_____

_____

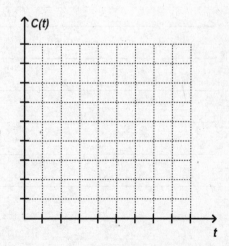

4. The profit produced by an apple orchard increases as more trees are planted. However, if the orchard becomes overcrowded, the trees will start to produce fewer apples, and the profit will start to decrease. The owner of a small apple orchard recorded the following approximate profit values $P(a)$ in the table below, where a is the number of apple trees in the orchard. Using the data in the table, identify where $P(a)$ is increasing and decreasing. Find when the owner earned the least profit and when the owner earned the most profit.

a	P(a)
0	0
10	1410
20	2380
30	3010
40	3220
50	3050
60	2400
70	1420
80	0

_____

_____

_____

_____

_____

_____

_____

_____

_____

_____

5. The absolute value function $y = |x|$ can be described using the following piecewise function.

$$f(x) = \begin{cases} -x, & x < 0 \\ x, & 0 \le x \end{cases}$$

a. Graph $f(x)$.

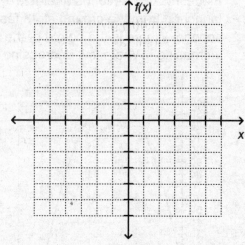

b. Where is the function decreasing and increasing?

_____

_____

_____

c. Where is $f(x)$ positive?

_____

_____

d. Explain why $f(x)$ is never negative.

_____

_____

_____

_____

_____

Name _____ Date _____ Class_____

The student will relate the domain of a function to its graph and to any quantitative relationship it describes.

SELECTED RESPONSE
Select the correct answer.

1. Circle the phrase that makes a true statement.

   The function $h(n)$ gives the number of person-hours it takes to assemble n engines in a factory. The most reasonable domain for $h(n)$ is

   | nonnegative rational numbers |
   | all real numbers |
   | nonnegative integers |
   | nonnegative real numbers |

2. The graph of the quadratic function $f(x)$ is shown below. What is the domain of $f(x)$?

   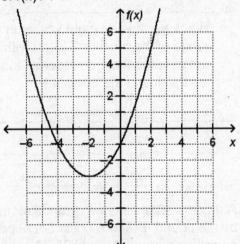

   Ⓐ The integers greater than –3.
   Ⓑ The real numbers greater than –3.
   Ⓒ The integers
   Ⓓ The real numbers

3. The growth of a population of bacteria can be modeled by an exponential function. The graph models the population of the bacteria colony $P(t)$ as a function of the time t, in weeks, that has passed. The initial population of the bacteria colony was 500. What is the domain of the function? What does the domain represent in this context?

   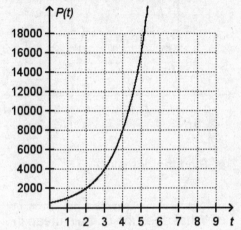

   Ⓐ The domain is the real numbers greater than 500. The domain represents the time, in weeks, that has passed.

   Ⓑ The domain is the real numbers greater than 500. The domain represents the population of the colony after a given number of weeks.

   Ⓒ The domain is the nonnegative real numbers. The domain represents the time, in weeks, that has passed.

   Ⓓ The domain is the nonnegative real numbers. The domain represents the population of the colony after a given number of weeks.

CONSTRUCTED RESPONSE

4. The function $h(t)$ describes the height, in feet, of an object at time t, in seconds, when it is launched upward from the ground at an initial speed of 112 feet per second.

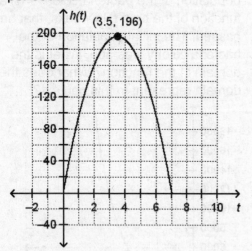

a. Find the domain.

_____

b. What does the domain mean in this context?

_____

_____

5. What are the domain and range of the exponential function $f(x)$?

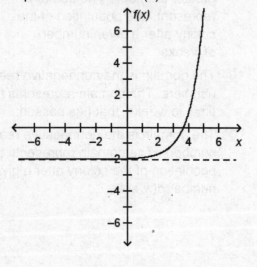

_____

_____

6. An electronics store sells a certain brand of tablet computer for $500. To stock the tablet computers, the store pays $150 per unit. The store also spends $1800 setting up a special display area to promote the product.

a. Write a function rule to describe the profit earned from selling the tablet computers. Note that profit is the revenue earned minus the cost.

_____

b. What is a reasonable domain for the function? Explain.

_____

_____

_____

_____

c. What are the first eight values in the range of the function? (Start with the range value that corresponds to the least value in the domain.)

_____

_____

_____

7. A grocery store sells two brands of ham by the pound. Brand A costs $4.19 per pound, and brand B costs $4.79 per pound. Brand A can be purchased at the deli in any amount, whereas brand B comes in prepackaged containers of either 0.5 pound or 1 pound. Write a function rule that represents the revenue earned for each of the brands and determine a reasonable domain for each. Explain your answers.

_____

_____

_____

_____

The student will use symbols or a table to find the average rate of change of functions and estimate rates from graphs.

SELECTED RESPONSE

Select the correct answer.

1. The table shows the height of a sassafras tree at each of two ages. What was the tree's average rate of growth during this time period?

Age (years)	Height (meters)
4	2
10	5

  Ⓐ 0.4 meter per year

  Ⓑ 0.5 meter per year

  Ⓒ 2 meters per year

  Ⓓ 2.5 meters per year

2. The graph shows the height h, in feet, of a football at time t, in seconds, from the moment it was kicked at ground level. Estimate the average rate of change in height from $t = 1.5$ seconds to $t = 1.75$ seconds.

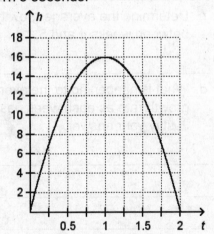

  Ⓐ −20 feet per second

  Ⓑ −12 feet per second

  Ⓒ 12 feet per second

  Ⓓ 20 feet per second

3. Find the average rate of change of the function $f(x) = 2\sqrt{x - 5} + 3$ from $x = 9$ to $x = 21$.

  Ⓐ −3   Ⓒ $\dfrac{1}{3}$

  Ⓑ $-\dfrac{1}{3}$ Ⓓ 3

Select all correct answers.

4. A person's body mass index (BMI) is calculated by dividing the person's mass in kilograms by the person's height in meters. The table shows the median BMI for U.S. males from age 2 to age 12. For which intervals is the average rate of change in the BMI positive?

Age (years)	Median BMI
2	16.575
4	15.641
6	15.367
8	15.769
10	16.625
12	17.788

  Ⓐ age 2 to age 4

  Ⓑ age 4 to age 6

  Ⓒ age 6 to age 8

  Ⓓ age 8 to age 10

  Ⓔ age 10 to age 12

5. Indicate whether each function's average rate of change on the interval $x = 0$ to $x = 2$ is greater than 2, less than 2, or equal to 2 by putting a check mark in the appropriate column of the table.

	Less	Equal	Greater
$f(x) = x + 2$			
$f(x) = 2x$			
$f(x) = \dfrac{5x}{2}$			
$f(x) = x^2$			
$f(x) = 2^x$			

CONSTRUCTED RESPONSE

6. The table gives the minutes of daylight on the first and last day of October 2012 for Anchorage, Alaska, and Los Angeles, California.

Location	Daylight on Oct. 1	Daylight on Oct. 31
Anchorage	686	517
Los Angeles	711	650

a. Calculate the average rate of change, in minutes per day, of daylight during October for each location.

_____

_____

b. Interpret your answers from part a. In other words, how are the day lengths changing in Anchorage and Los Angeles in October?

_____

_____

_____

_____

_____

_____

c. The sun rises at 7:00 A.M. on October 17, 2012, in Los Angeles. Estimate the time at which the sun sets that day. Explain your reasoning and show your work.

_____

_____

_____

_____

_____

_____

7. The graph models the population $P(t)$ of a bacteria colony as a function of time t, in weeks.

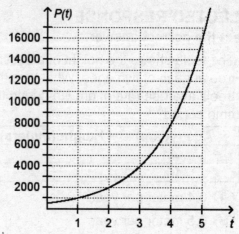

a. Determine the average growth rate between weeks 2 and 3.

_____

b. Determine the average growth rate between weeks 3 and 4.

_____

c. Determine the average growth rate between weeks 4 and 5.

_____

d. What is happening to the average growth rate as each week passes? Justify your answer.

_____

_____

_____

_____

e. What do you think the average growth rate will be between weeks 5 and 6 if the pattern continues?

_____

_____

_____

_____

Name _____ Date _____ Class_____

The student will graph linear and quadratic functions and show intercepts, maxima, and minima.

SELECTED RESPONSE
Select the correct answer.

1. Circle the values that make a true statement.

   In the linear function shown, the *x*-intercept

   is
   | -2 |
   | 2 |
   | -4 |
   | 4 |

   and the *y*-intercept is

   | -2 |
   | 2 |
   | -4 |
   | 4 |
   .

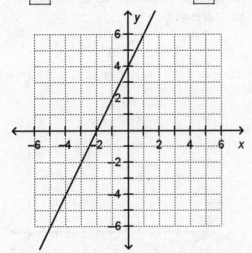

2. What is the vertex of the quadratic function *f(x)*? Is it a maximum or a minimum?

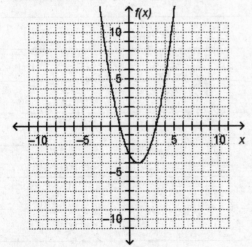

   Ⓐ (1, –4); minimum

   Ⓑ (0, –3); minimum

   Ⓒ (–1, 0); minimum

   Ⓓ (3, 0); maximum

CONSTRUCTED RESPONSE

3. Sally decides to make and sell necklaces to earn money to buy a new computer. She plans to charge $5.25 per necklace.

   a. Write a function that describes the revenue *R(n)*, in dollars, Sally will earn from selling *n* necklaces.

   _____

   b. What is a reasonable domain for this function?

   _____
   _____
   _____

   c. Graph the function.

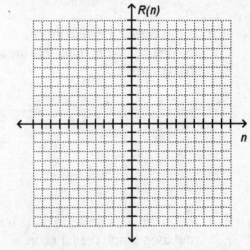

   d. Identify and interpret the intercepts of the function.

   _____
   _____
   _____
   _____
   _____
   _____
   _____
   _____

Name _____ Date _____ Class_____

4. The function $h(t) = -4.9t^2 + 24.5t$ models the height $h(t)$, in meters, of an object t seconds after it is thrown upward from the ground with an initial velocity of 24.5 meters per second.

a. Calculate and interpret the intercepts of the function.

_____

_____

_____

_____

b. Calculate the vertex of the function.

_____

_____

_____

_____

c. Is the vertex a minimum or a maximum? What does this mean in this context?

_____

_____

_____

_____

d. Plot the points found in parts a and b and then graph the function.

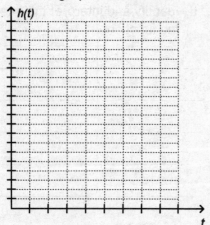

5. A farmer has 1200 feet of fencing to enclose a square area for his horses and a rectangular area for his pigs. The farmer decides that the enclosures should share a full side to maximize the usefulness of the fencing. He also wants to maximize the combined area of the enclosures. Write a function that describes the combined area of the enclosures $A(s)$ as a function of the side length s of the square enclosure. Then, graph the function to determine dimensions of each enclosure that maximize the combined area. Explain your answer.

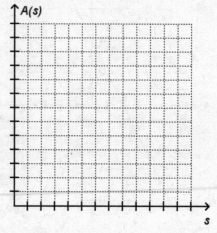

_____

_____

_____

_____

_____

_____

_____

_____

_____

_____

_____

_____

Name _____ Date _____ Class_____

The student will graph functions: square root, cube root, and piecewise-defined, including step and absolute value.

SELECTED RESPONSE
Select the correct answer.

1. What kind of function best describes the following graph?

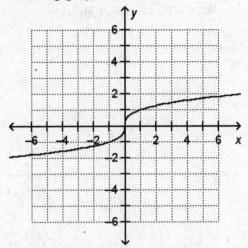

Ⓐ An absolute value function

Ⓑ A cube root function

Ⓒ A square root function

Ⓓ A step function

2. The graph of $f(x)$ is shown below.

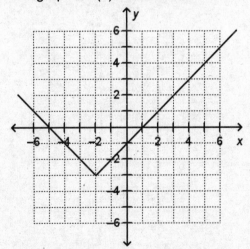

Indicate the x- and y-intercepts of $f(x)$ by putting a check mark in the appropriate column of the table.

	1	−1	5	−5
x-intercept(s)				
y-intercept(s)				

3. What is the vertex of $f(x)$? Is it a maximum or a minimum?

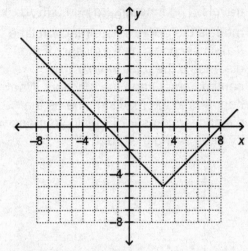

Ⓐ (0, −2); minimum

Ⓑ (3, −5); minimum

Ⓒ (−2, 0); minimum

Ⓓ (8, 0); maximum

CONSTRUCTED RESPONSE

4. Graph the piecewise defined function. What are the domain and range?

$$f(x) = \begin{cases} -2 & x < -3 \\ 1 & -3 \le x < 1 \\ 4 & x \ge 1 \end{cases}$$

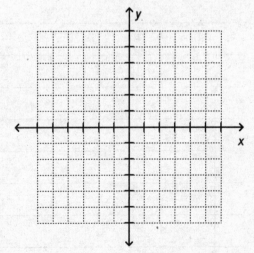

_____

_____

5. A simple reaction time test involves dropping a meter-long ruler between someone's thumb and index finger and measuring the time it takes for the person to catch it against the distance the ruler travels. The function $t(d) = 0.045\sqrt{d}$ models the approximate reaction time $t(d)$, in seconds, as a function of the distance d the ruler travels, in centimeters. Graph the function. What happens to the reaction time as the distance increases? Explain your answer by interpreting the graph.

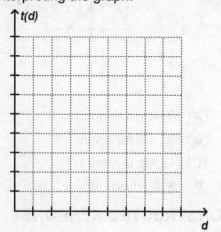

_____

_____

_____

_____

_____

_____

_____

_____

_____

_____

_____

6. Write and graph a piecewise-defined step function $f(x)$ that has the following characteristics.

I. $f(x)$ has more than one x-intercept

II. The domain of $f(x)$ is the real numbers

III. The range of $f(x)$ consists of four unique integers

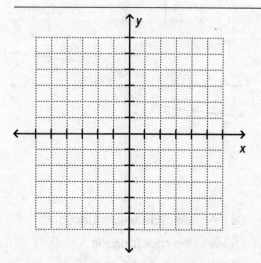

7. Graph the function $f(x) = 2\sqrt[3]{x-6} + 4$ Find the intervals where the function is increasing and decreasing.

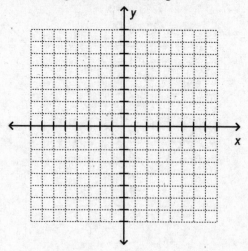

_____

_____

_____

_____

Name _____ Date _____ Class_____

The student will graph exponential functions, showing intercepts and end behavior.

SELECTED RESPONSE
Select the correct answer.

1. The exponential function $f(x)$ has a horizontal asymptote at $y = 3$. What is the end behavior of $f(x)$?

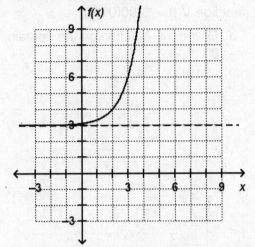

Ⓐ As x decreases without bound, $f(x)$ decreases without bound. As x increases without bound, $f(x)$ increases without bound.

Ⓑ As x decreases without bound, $f(x)$ increases without bound. As x increases without bound, $f(x)$ decreases without bound.

Ⓒ As x decreases without bound, $f(x)$ approaches, but never reaches, 3. As x increases without bound, $f(x)$ increases without bound.

Ⓓ As x decreases without bound, $f(x)$ decreases without bound. As x increases without bound, $f(x)$ approaches, but never reaches, 4.

2. A website allows its users to submit and edit content in an online encyclopedia. The graph shows the number of articles $a(t)$ in the encyclopedia t months after the website goes live. How many articles were in the encyclopedia when it went live?

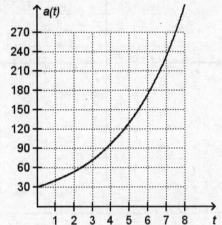

Ⓐ 0   Ⓒ 60

Ⓑ 30   Ⓓ 180

Select all correct answers.

3. Which statements are true about the graph of the exponential function $f(x)$?

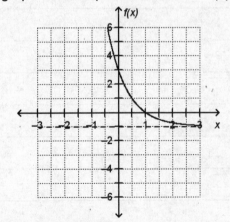

Ⓐ The domain is all real numbers.

Ⓑ The range is all real numbers.

Ⓒ The $f(x)$-intercept is 3.

Ⓓ The x-intercept is −1.

Ⓔ As x increases without bound, $f(x)$ approaches, but never reaches, −1.

CONSTRUCTED RESPONSE

4. Suppose an exponential function has a domain of all real numbers and a range that is bounded by an integer. How many *x*-intercepts could such a function have? Graph examples to support your answer.

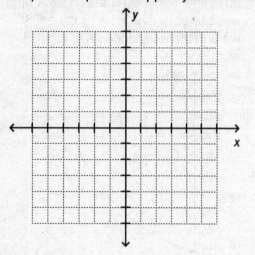

_____

_____

_____

_____

_____

_____

_____

_____

_____

_____

_____

_____

_____

_____

5. The value of an object decreases from its purchase price over time. This change in value can be modeled using an exponential function. A new copy machine purchased by a school for $1200 has an estimated useful life span of 12 years. After 12 years, the copier is worth $250. The value $V(t)$ of the copier after t years is approximated by the function $V(t) = 1200(0.88)^t$.

a. Graph the function on the domain $0 \le t \le 12$.

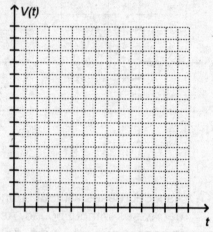

b. Estimate and interpret the $V(t)$-intercept.

_____

_____

_____

_____

_____

_____

_____

_____

_____

_____

_____

The student will factor and complete the square to show zeros, extreme values, and symmetry of a graph in context.

SELECTED RESPONSE
Select the correct answer.

1. What are the zeros of the function $f(x) = x^2 + 2x - 8$?
   - (A) $x = 4$ and $x = -2$
   - (B) $x = -4$ and $x = 2$
   - (C) $x = -4$ and $x = -2$
   - (D) $x = 4$ and $x = 2$

2. What is the axis of symmetry of the graph of $f(x) = 3x^2 - 6x + 6$?
   - (A) $x = -1$
   - (B) $x = 1$
   - (C) $y = 1$
   - (D) $y = 3$

Select all correct answers.

3. Which of the following statements correctly describe the graph of $f(x) = 2x^2 + 8x - 2$?
   - (A) The maximum value of the function is 10.
   - (B) The minimum value of the function is −10.
   - (C) The axis of symmetry is the line $x = -2$.
   - (D) The axis of symmetry is the line $x = 2$.
   - (E) The graph is a parabola that opens up.
   - (F) The graph is a parabola that opens down.

4. Consider the function $f(x) = 2x^2 + 4x - 30$. Indicate whether each statement is true or false by putting a check mark in the appropriate column of the table.

	True	False
The vertex of the graph is (1, −32).		
The zeros are 3 and −5.		
The graph opens down.		
The axis of symmetry is $x = -1$.		
The y-intercept is −30.		

CONSTRUCTED RESPONSE

5. Consider the function $f(x) = 4x^2 + 4x - 15$.

   a. Factor the expression $4x^2 + 4x - 15$. What are the zeros of $f(x)$?

   _____

   _____

   _____

   b. What are the coordinates of the vertex of $f(x)$? Is the vertex the maximum or minimum value of the function? Explain.

   _____

   _____

6. The axis of symmetry for a quadratic function is a vertical line halfway between the x-intercepts of the function. Miguel says that the graph of $f(x) = -2x^2 - 16x - 34$ has no axis of symmetry because the function has no x-intercepts.

   a. Explain why Miguel is incorrect.

   _____

   _____

   _____

   _____

   _____

   _____

   _____

   _____

   _____

   b. Find the axis of symmetry of the graph of $f(x)$. Show your work.

   _____

   _____

   _____

   _____

   _____

   _____

   _____

   _____

7. The arch that supports a bridge that passes over a river forms a parabola whose height above the water level is given by $h(x) = -\dfrac{9}{125}x^2 + 45$, where $x = 0$ represents the center of the bridge. The distance between the sides of the arch at the water level is the same as the length of the bridge.

   a. How long is the bridge? Explain.

   _____

   _____

   _____

   _____

   _____

   _____

   _____

   _____

   _____

   b. A sailboat with a mast that extends 50 feet above the water is sailing down the river. Will the sailboat be able to pass under the bridge? Explain.

   _____

   _____

   _____

   _____

   _____

   _____

   _____

   _____

The student will use properties of exponents to interpret expressions for exponential functions.

SELECTED RESPONSE
Select the correct answer.

1. The balance B, in dollars, after t years of an investment that earns interest compounded annually is given by the function $B(t) = 1500(1.045)^t$. To the nearest hundredth of a percent, what is the monthly interest rate for the investment?

   (A) 0.37%   (C) 4.50%

   (B) 3.67%   (D) 69.59%

2. After t days, the mass m, in grams, of 100 grams of a certain radioactive element is given by the function $m(t) = 100(0.97)^t$. To the nearest percent, what is the weekly decay rate of the element?

   (A) 3%   (C) 21%

   (B) 19%   (D) 81%

Select all correct answers.

3. Which of these functions describe exponential growth?

   (A) $f(t) = 1.25^t$

   (B) $f(t) = 2(0.93)^{0.5t}$

   (C) $f(t) = 3(1.07)^{3t}$

   (D) $f(t) = 18(0.85)^t$

   (E) $f(t) = 0.5(1.05)^t$

   (F) $f(t) = 3(1.71)^{5t}$

   (G) $f(t) = 0.68^{2t}$

   (H) $f(t) = 8(1.56)^{1.4t}$

Select the correct answer for each lettered part.

4. Determine if each function below is equivalent to $f(t) = 0.25^t$.

   a. $f(t) = 1^{\frac{t}{4}}$ ○ Equivalent   ○ Not equivalent

   b. $f(t) = 0.5^{2t}$ ○ Equivalent   ○ Not equivalent

   c. $f(t) = 0.0625^{\frac{t}{2}}$ ○ Equivalent   ○ Not equivalent

   d. $f(t) = 0.125^{\frac{t}{2}}$ ○ Equivalent   ○ Not equivalent

   e. $f(t) = 4^{-t}$ ○ Equivalent   ○ Not equivalent

   f. $f(t) = -0.25^{-t}$ ○ Equivalent   ○ Not equivalent

CONSTRUCTED RESPONSE

5. The population P, in millions, of a certain country can be modeled by the function $P(t) = 3.98(1.02)^t$, where t is the number of years after 1990.

   a. Write the equation in the form $P(t) = a(1 + r)^t$.

_____

   b. What is the value of r in your answer from part a? What does this value represent?

_____

_____

Name _____ Date _____ Class_____

6. How do the function values of $g(x) = 200(4^{x-1})$ compare to the corresponding function values of $f(x) = 200(4^x)$? Explain using a transformation of $g(x)$.

_____
_____
_____
_____
_____
_____
_____
_____

7. The value V, in dollars, after t years of an investment that earns interest compounded annually is given by the function $V(t) = 1500(1.035)^t$.

a. Rewrite $V(t)$ to find the annual interest rate of the investment.

_____
_____
_____

b. Find the approximate interest rate over a 5-year period by rewriting the function using the power of a power property. Round to the nearest percent.

_____
_____
_____

8. Sanjay plans to deposit $850 in a bank account whose balance B, in dollars, after t years is modeled by $B(t) = 850(1.04)^t$.

a. Write the equation in the form $B(t) = a(1 + r)^t$. What is the annual interest rate of Sanjay's account?

_____
_____
_____
_____
_____

b. Rewrite the equation from part a to approximate the monthly interest rate. Round to the nearest hundredth of a percent.

_____
_____
_____
_____

c. Rebecca deposits $850 in a bank account that earns 0.35% interest compounded monthly. Without calculating the account balances, which account will have a larger balance after 6 months? Explain.

_____
_____
_____
_____

The student will compare functions represented differently (algebraically, graphically, in tables, or by description).

SELECTED RESPONSE
Select the correct answer.

1. Circle the function that makes a true statement.

   A function that has the same domain as the quadratic function shown is

   $$f(x) = \sqrt{x-2}$$
   $$g(x) = \sqrt{x} - 2$$
   $$h(x) = |x-2|$$
   $$k(x) = 3^x, \ x \geq -2$$

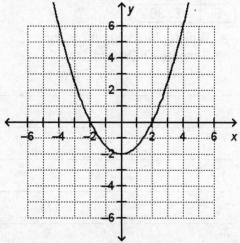

2. The function $f(x)$ is defined for only the values given in the table. Which function has the same x-intercepts as $f(x)$?

x	$f(x)$
-2	2.5
-1	0
0	-1.5
1	-2
2	-1.5
3	0
4	2.5

   Ⓐ $g(x) = 2x + 2$

   Ⓑ $h(x) = -\dfrac{1}{3}x + 2$

   Ⓒ $j(x) = x^2 + 2x - 3$

   Ⓓ $k(x) = |x-1| - 2$

Select all correct answers.

3. Which functions have the same range as the cube root function $f(x)$ shown in the graph?

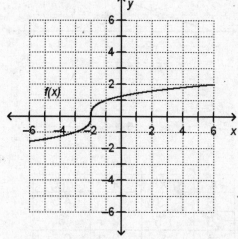

   Ⓐ $g(x) = \sqrt{x+2}$

   Ⓑ $h(x) = \dfrac{1}{3}x + 1$

   Ⓒ $j(x) = x^2 - 6x + 8$

   Ⓓ $k(x) = -|2x| - 1$

   Ⓔ $m(x) = \sqrt[3]{2x-1} + 2$

CONSTRUCTED RESPONSE

4. The function $f(x)$ is defined for only the values in the table. Let $g(x) = x^2 + 3$ for all real numbers $1 \leq x \leq 4$. Compare the domains, ranges, and initial values of the functions.

x	$f(x)$
1	4
2	6
3	10
4	18

_____

_____

_____

_____

Name _____ Date _____ Class_____

5. Which of the functions described below has a greater maximum value on the domain $-6 \le x \le 6$? Explain.

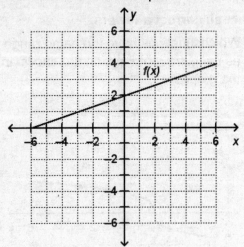

x	g(x)	x	g(x)
−6	−13	1	4.5
−5	−7.5	2	3
−4	−3	3	0.5
−3	0.5	4	−3
−2	3	5	−7.5
−1	4.5	6	−13
0	5		

_____

_____

_____

_____

_____

_____

_____

_____

_____

_____

_____

6. A company offers two cell phone plans to its employees. The function $A(t) = 70t$ gives the cost, in dollars, of cell phone plan A for t months. Plan B allows an employee to receive an additional discount by paying for a certain number of months in advance. The table describes the function $B(t)$, which gives the cost, in dollars, of cell phone plan B for t months.

t	B(t)
1	$70
2	$140
3	$200
4	$250
5	$290
6	$330

a. Which plan costs more for 3 months? Explain.

_____

_____

_____

_____

_____

_____

_____

b. After how many months will an employee on plan B be saving more than $50 over an employee on plan A? Explain.

_____

_____

_____

_____

_____

_____

_____

_____

Name _____ Date _____ Class_____

The student will determine an explicit expression, a recursive process, or steps for calculation from a context.

SELECTED RESPONSE
Select the correct answer.

1. A small swimming pool initially contains 400 gallons of water, and water is being added at a rate of 10 gallons per minute. Which expression represents the volume of the pool after t minutes?

   (A) $-10t + 400$

   (B) $10t + 400$

   (C) $400t + 10$

   (D) $400(1.10)^t$

2. A diver jumps off a 10-meter-high diving board with an initial vertical velocity of 3 meters per second. The function $h(t) = -4.9t^2 + v_0 t + h_0$ models the height of a falling object, where v_0 is the initial vertical velocity and h_0 is the initial height. Use the numbers given below to write the function that models the diver's height h, in meters, above the water at time t, in seconds.

   $h(t) = -4.9t^2$ [ ] [ ] t [ ] [ ]

   | + | – | 10 | 3 | 7 | 13 |

3. Andrea buys a car for \$16,000. The car loses value at a rate of 8% each year. Which recursive rule below describes the value of Andrea's car V, in dollars, after t years?

   (A) $V(0) = \$16,000$ and
   $V(t) = 0.08 \cdot V(t-1)$ for $t \geq 1$

   (B) $V(0) = \$16,000$ and
   $V(t) = 0.2 \cdot V(t-1)$ for $t \geq 1$

   (C) $V(0) = \$16,000$ and
   $V(t) = 0.92 \cdot V(t-1)$ for $t \geq 1$

   (D) $V(0) = \$16,000$ and
   $V(t) = 1.08 \cdot V(t-1)$ for $t \geq 1$

Select all correct answers.

4. Miguel has \$250 dollars saved, and he adds \$5 to his savings every week. Which functions describe the amount A, in dollars, that Miguel has saved after t weeks?

   (A) $A(t) = 5t + 250$

   (B) $A(t) = -5t + 250$

   (C) $A(t) = 250t + 5$

   (D) $A(0) = 250$ and $A(t) = A(t-1) + 5$ for $t \geq 1$

   (E) $A(0) = 250$ and $A(t+1) = A(t) + 5$ for $t \geq 0$

   (F) $A(0) = 250$ and $A(t+1) = 5A(t)$ for $t \geq 0$

CONSTRUCTED RESPONSE

5. When a piece of paper is folded in half, the total thickness doubles and the total area is halved. Suppose you have a sheet of paper that is 0.1 mm thick and has an area of 10,000 mm^2.

   a. Write an equation that models the thickness T, in millimeters, of the sheet of paper after it has been folded n times.

   _____

   _____

   _____

   _____

   b. Write an equation that models the area A, in square millimeters, of the sheet of paper after it has been folded n times.

   _____

   _____

   _____

   _____

6. The people at a conference use the following exercise to get to know each other. The leader of the conference chooses 4 people, greets each of them with a handshake, and they chat. After one minute, those 4 people each choose 4 people, greet each with a handshake, and chat. This continues until each person at the conference has shaken someone's hand. Write an exponential function that models the number of handshakes H in the nth minute.

_____

7. A population of 300 sea turtles grows by 5% each year.

   a. Describe the steps needed to calculate the population each year.

_____

_____

_____

_____

_____

_____

_____

_____

_____

   b. Write a recursive function for the population P after t years.

_____

_____

8. Simon wants to use 500 feet of fencing to enclose a rectangular area in his backyard.

   a. Write a function for the enclosed area A, in square feet, in terms of the width w, in feet. Show your work.

_____

_____

_____

_____

_____

_____

_____

_____

_____

_____

   b. What are the dimensions of the largest rectangle Simon can enclose with 500 feet of fencing? Explain.

_____

_____

_____

_____

_____

_____

_____

_____

The student will combine standard function types using arithmetic operations.

SELECTED RESPONSE
Select the correct answer.

1. A rectangle has side lengths $(x + 4)$ feet and $(2x + 1)$ feet for $x > 0$. Write a function that describes the area A, in square feet, in terms of x.

   (A) $A(x) = 3x + 5$

   (B) $A(x) = 6x + 10$

   (C) $A(x) = 2x^2 + 9x + 4$

   (D) $A(x) = 2x^2 + 7x - 4$

2. In a factory, the cost of producing n items is $C(n) = 25n + 150$. Which function describes the average cost of producing one item when n items are produced?

   (A) $A(n) = 25n + 150$

   (B) $A(n) = 25 + \dfrac{150}{n}$

   (C) $A(n) = 25n^2 + 150n$

   (D) $A(n) = \dfrac{25}{n} + \dfrac{150}{n^2}$

Select all correct answers.

3. Two identical water tanks each hold 10,000 liters. Tank A starts full, but water is leaking out at a rate of 10 liters per minute. Tank B starts empty and is filled at a rate of 13 liters per minute. Which functions correctly describe the combined volume V of both tanks after t minutes?

   (A) $V(t) = 10,000 - 10t + 13t$

   (B) $V(t) = 10,000 - 10t - 13t$

   (C) $V(t) = 10,000 + 10t - 13t$

   (D) $V(t) = 10,000 - 3t$

   (E) $V(t) = 10,000 + 3t$

   (F) $V(t) = 10,000 - 23t$

Select the correct answer for each lettered part.

4. Let $f(x) = x^2 - x - 2$ and $g(x) = x^2 + x - 6$. Classify each function below as linear, quadratic, or neither.

   a. $f(x) + g(x)$ ○ Linear   ○ Quadratic   ○ Neither

   b. $f(x) - g(x)$ ○ Linear   ○ Quadratic   ○ Neither

   c. $\dfrac{f(x)}{g(x)}$ ○ Linear   ○ Quadratic   ○ Neither

   d. $f(x) \cdot g(x)$ ○ Linear   ○ Quadratic   ○ Neither

CONSTRUCTED RESPONSE

5. Let $f(x) = x^2 + x - 6$ and $g(x) = x^2 - 4$. Find $f(x) + g(x)$ and $f(x) - g(x)$. Simplify your answers.

_____

_____

_____

_____

6. Esther exercises for 45 minutes. She rides her bike at 880 feet per minute for t minutes and then jogs at 400 feet per minute for the rest of the time.

   a. Write a function that describes the distance d_1, in feet, that Esther travels while riding her bike for t minutes.

   _____

   b. Write a function that describes the distance d_2, in feet, that Esther travels while jogging.

   _____

   c. Use your answers from parts a and b to write a function that describes the distance d, in feet, that Esther travels while exercising.

   _____

   _____

7. Trina deposits $1500 in an account that earns 5% interest compounded annually. Pablo deposits $1800 in an account that earns 2.5% interest compounded annually. Write a function that models the difference D, in dollars, between the balance of Trina's account and the balance of Pablo's account after t years. (Hint: The difference between the two balances should always be positive.)

   _____

   _____

   _____

   _____

   _____

   _____

8. Town A and town B both had a population of 15,000 people in the year 2000. The population of town A increased by 2.5% each year. The population of town B decreased by 3.5% each year.

   a. Write a function $A(t)$, the population of town A t years after 2000.

   _____

   b. Write a function for $B(t)$, the population of town B t years after 2000.

   _____

   c. Find $A(t) + B(t)$ and $\dfrac{A(t)}{B(t)}$. Simplify your answers and interpret each function in terms of the situation. If necessary, round decimals to the nearest thousandth.

   _____

   _____

   _____

   _____

   _____

   _____

   _____

   _____

   _____

   _____

   _____

   _____

   _____

   _____

   _____

The student will write arithmetic and geometric sequences both recursively and explicitly, and use them to model.

SELECTED RESPONSE

Select the correct answer.

1. A theater has 18 rows of seats. There are 22 seats in the first row, 26 seats in the second row, 30 seats in the third row, and so on. Which of the following is a recursive formula for the arithmetic sequence that represents this situation?

   (A) $f(0) = 18$, $f(n) = f(n-1) + 4$
   for $1 \leq n \leq 18$

   (B) $f(1) = 22$, $f(n) = f(n-1) + 4$
   for $2 \leq n \leq 18$

   (C) $f(n) = 18 + 4n$

   (D) $f(n) = 22 + 4(n-1)$

2. The table below shows the balance b, in dollars, of Daryl's savings account t years after he made an initial deposit. What is an explicit formula for the geometric sequence that represents this situation?

Time, t (years)	Balance, b (dollars)
1	$1218
2	$1236.27
3	$1254.81
4	$1273.64

   (A) $b(t) = 1.015(1218)^{t-1}$

   (B) $b(t) = 1218(1.015)^t$

   (C) $b(t) = 1218 + 1.015(t-1)$

   (D) $b(t) = 1218(1.015)^{t-1}$

Select all correct answers.

3. Amelia earns $36,000 in the first year from her new job and earns a 6% raise each year. Which of the following models Amelia's pay p, in dollars, in year t of her job?

   (A) $p(0) = 36,000$, $p(t) = 1.06 \cdot p(t-1)$
   for $t \geq 1$

   (B) $p(1) = 36,000$, $p(t) = 1.06 \cdot p(t-1)$
   for $t \geq 2$

   (C) $p(t) = 36,000 \cdot 1.06^{t-1}$ for $t \geq 1$

   (D) $p(t) = 1.06 \cdot 36,000^{t-1}$ for $t \geq 1$

   (E) $p(t) = 1.06(t-1) + 36,000$ for $t \geq 1$

   (F) $p(t) = 38,160 \cdot 1.06^{t-2}$ for $t \geq 1$

CONSTRUCTED RESPONSE

4. Calvin is practicing the trumpet for an audition to play in a band. He starts practicing the trumpet 40 minutes the first day and then increases his practice time by 5 minutes per day. The audition is on the 10th day.

   a. Write a recursive rule that represents the time t, in minutes, Calvin practices on day d.

   _____

   _____

   b. Write an explicit rule that represents the time t, in minutes, Calvin practices on day d.

   _____

   _____

   c. Use the result from part b to find how long Calvin practices on the 8th day. Show your work.

   _____

   _____

   _____

5. The table displays the speed of a car s, in feet per second, t seconds after it starts coasting.

Time, t (seconds)	Speed, s (ft/sec)
1	57
2	54.15
3	51.44
4	48.87

a. Explain why this sequence is geometric.

_____

_____

_____

_____

_____

b. Write an explicit rule for this sequence using the values from the table.

_____

_____

c. Use the result from part b to write a recursive rule for this sequence.

_____

_____

d. What is the speed of the car when it begins to coast? Show your work.

_____

_____

_____

_____

6. The table below shows the cost c, in dollars, of a private party on a boat based on the number of people p attending.

People, p	Cost, c (dollars)
2	306
3	334
4	362
5	390

a. Does an arithmetic sequence or a geometric sequence model this situation? Justify your answer by using the values in the table.

_____

_____

_____

_____

_____

b. Write an explicit formula and a recursive formula for the sequence. Show your work.

_____

_____

_____

_____

c. How much would it cost for 44 people to attend the private party? Show your work.

_____

_____

_____

_____

_____

_____

Name _____ Date _____ Class_____

The student will identify the effect of a transformation on the graph of $f(x)$ and write an equation of a transformed graph.

SELECTED RESPONSE

Select all correct answers.

1. The graph of $g(x)$ is shown below. Use the numbers given below to write the function $g(x)$ that can be obtained by applying horizontal and vertical shifts to the parent function $f(x) = \sqrt[3]{x}$.

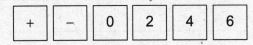

$$g(x) = \sqrt[3]{x\ \boxed{}\ \boxed{}}\ \boxed{}\ \boxed{}$$

+	−	0	2	4	6

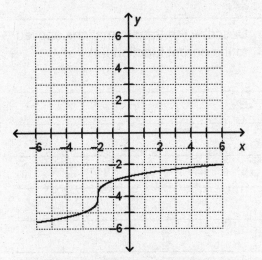

Select the correct answer.

2. What must be done to the graph of $f(x) = |x|$ to obtain the graph of the function $g(x) = 0.5|x + 4| - 10$?

Ⓐ The graph of $f(x)$ is shifted left 4 units, horizontally shrunk by a factor of 0.5, and shifted down 10 units.

Ⓑ The graph of $f(x)$ is shifted right 4 units, vertically shrunk by a factor of 0.5, and shifted down 10 units.

Ⓒ The graph of $f(x)$ is shifted left 4 units, vertically shrunk by a factor of 0.5, and shifted down 10 units.

Ⓓ The graph of $f(x)$ is shifted left 4 units, vertically shrunk by a factor of 0.5, and shifted up 10 units.

CONSTRUCTED RESPONSE

3. Describe the transformations applied to the graph of the parent function $f(x) = \sqrt{x}$ used to graph $g(x) = -2\sqrt{1-x} + 3$. Graph $g(x)$.

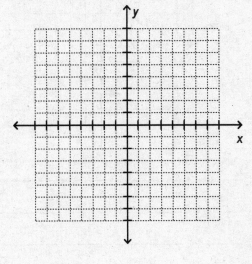

_____
_____
_____
_____
_____
_____

4. Describe how the nonzero slope m of a linear function $g(x) = mx$ is a transformation of the graph of the parent linear function $f(x) = x$.

_____
_____
_____
_____
_____
_____

5. For the following graphs of transformed functions, state the parent function $f(x)$, the type of transformation, and write a function rule.

a.

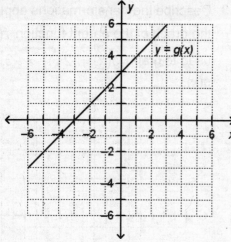

_____

_____

_____

_____

_____

b.

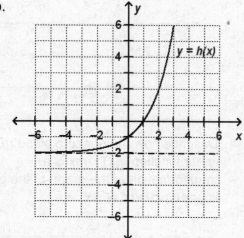

_____

_____

_____

_____

6. a. Rewrite $g(x) = -\frac{1}{2}x^2 - 2x + 2$ in vertex form. Show your work.

_____

_____

_____

_____

_____

_____

_____

_____

b. Describe the transformations applied to the parent function $f(x) = x^2$.

_____

_____

_____

_____

_____

_____

_____

_____

c. Graph $g(x)$.

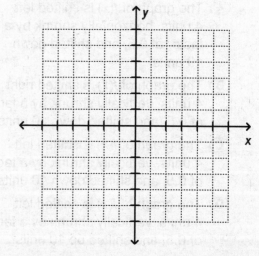

The student will solve $f(x) = c$ for a simple function f that has an inverse and write an expression for the inverse.

SELECTED RESPONSE

Select the correct answer.

1. What is the inverse of $f(x) = -2x + 6$?

   Ⓐ $g(x) = \dfrac{1}{2}x - 3$

   Ⓑ $g(x) = -\dfrac{1}{2}x + 3$

   Ⓒ $g(x) = 2x - 6$

   Ⓓ $g(x) = -\dfrac{1}{2}x + 6$

2. The point (2, 12) is on the graph of $f(x)$. Which of the following points must be on the graph of $g(x)$, the inverse of $f(x)$?

   Ⓐ $(-2, 12)$
   Ⓑ $(2, -12)$
   Ⓒ $(2, 12)$
   Ⓓ $(12, 2)$

Select all correct answers.

3. If $f(x) = -\dfrac{1}{8}x + 5$, which of the following statements about $g(x)$, the inverse of $f(x)$, are true?

   Ⓐ $g(-2.125) = 57$
   Ⓑ $g(-0.5) = 44$
   Ⓒ $g(-0.375) = 37$
   Ⓓ $g(0.125) = 39$
   Ⓔ $g(0.625) = 45$
   Ⓕ $g(1.125) = 40$

CONSTRUCTED RESPONSE

4. Let $f(x) = -13x + 52$. Find the inverse of $f(x)$ and use it to find a value of x such that $f(x) = 182$. Show your work.

   _____

   _____

   _____

   _____

   _____

   _____

5. At a carnival, you pay $15 for admission, plus $3 for each ride you go on.

   a. Write a function $A(r)$ that models the amount A, in dollars, you would spend to ride r rides at the carnival.

   _____

   b. Find the inverse of $A(r)$. Show your work.

   _____

   _____

   _____

   _____

   _____

   c. What does the inverse function found in part b represent in the context of the problem?

   _____

   _____

   _____

   _____

6. The graph of $f(x) = 3x - 6$ is shown, along with the dashed line $y = x$.

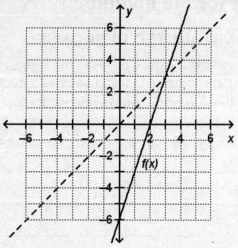

a. Find $g(x)$, the inverse of $f(x)$. Show your work.

_____

_____

_____

_____

_____

_____

_____

_____

_____

_____

_____

b. Graph $g(x)$ on the coordinate grid above.

c. How are the graphs of $f(x)$ and $g(x)$ related to the line $y = x$?

_____

_____

_____

7. a. Find $g(x)$, the inverse of $f(x) = mx + b$. Show your work.

_____

_____

_____

_____

_____

_____

_____

_____

_____

_____

_____

b. Use the formula for $g(x)$ to find the inverse of $f(x) = 4x + 11$.

_____

c. Does every linear function have an inverse? Use your result from part a to explain why or why not. If not, give the general forms of any linear functions that do not.

_____

_____

_____

_____

_____

_____

_____

_____

_____

_____

The student will prove that linear functions grow by equal differences while exponential functions by equal factors.

SELECTED RESPONSE
Select the correct answer.

1. For some exponential function $f(x)$, $f(0) = 12$, $f(1) = 18$, and $f(2) = 27$. How does $f(x)$ change when x increases by 1?

   Ⓐ $f(x)$ grows by a factor of $\frac{2}{3}$.

   Ⓑ $f(x)$ grows by a factor of $\frac{3}{2}$.

   Ⓒ $f(x)$ increases by 6.

   Ⓓ $f(x)$ increases by 9.

2. The balance B of an account earning simple interest is $1000 when the account is opened, $1075 after one year, and $1150 after two years. How does the balance of the account change from one year to the next?

   Ⓐ The balance increases by 7.5%.

   Ⓑ The balance decreases by 7.5%.

   Ⓒ The balance increases by $75.

   Ⓓ The balance increases by $150.

Select all correct answers.

3. Marco starts reading a 350-page book at 9 a.m. The number of pages P Marco has left to read t hours after 9 a.m. is modeled by the function $P(t) = 350 - 45t$. During which of the following time periods does Marco read the same number of pages he reads between 11 a.m. and 1 p.m.?

   Ⓐ 9 a.m. to 11 a.m.

   Ⓑ 11 a.m. to 12 noon

   Ⓒ 12:30 p.m. to 1:30 p.m.

   Ⓓ 2 p.m. to 4 p.m.

   Ⓔ 1:30 p.m. to 3.30 p.m.

Match each statement in the proof with the correct reason.

Using the list of reasons below, write the correct reason for each statement.

Statements		Reasons
4. $x_2 - x_1 = x_4 - x_3, f(x) = ab^x$	4.	
5. $b^{x_2 - x_1} = b^{x_4 - x_3}$	5.	
6. $\dfrac{b^{x_2}}{b^{x_1}} = \dfrac{b^{x_4}}{b^{x_3}}$	6.	
7. $\dfrac{ab^{x_2}}{ab^{x_1}} = \dfrac{ab^{x_4}}{ab^{x_3}}$	7.	
8. $\dfrac{f(x_2)}{f(x_1)} = \dfrac{f(x_4)}{f(x_3)}$	8.	

Given	Definition of $f(x)$
Power of Powers Property	Quotient of Powers Property
Distributive Property	If $x = y$, then $b^x = b^y$
Subtraction Property of Equality	Multiplication Property of Equality

Name _____ Date _____ Class_____

CONSTRUCTED RESPONSE

9. Complete the reasoning to prove that linear functions grow by equal differences over equal intervals.

   Given: $x_2 - x_1 = x_4 - x_3$

   $f(x)$ is a linear function of the form $f(x) = mx + b$.

   Prove: $f(x_2) - f(x_1) = f(x_4) - f(x_3)$

$x_2 - x_1 = x_4 - x_3$	Given
$m(x_2 - x_1) = m(x_4 - x_3)$	_____
$mx_2 - mx_1 = mx_4 - mx_3$	_____
$mx_2 + b - mx_1 - b = mx_4 + \underline{} - mx_3 - \underline{}$	Addition and subtraction properties
$(mx_2 + b) - (mx_1 + b) = \underline{}$	Distributive property
$f(x_2) - f(x_1) = \underline{}$	Definition of $f(x)$

10. Sandra's annual salary S, in dollars, after working at the same company for t years is given by the function $S(t) = 38{,}000 + 1500t$.

    a. Complete the table showing Sandra's salary after each year for the first five years.

Time, t (years)	Salary, S (dollars)
1	
2	
3	
4	
5	

    b. Show that Sandra's salary increases by the same amount each year.

    _____

    _____

    _____

    _____

    _____

    _____

    _____

    _____

    _____

11. The population of a certain town is 3500 people in 2000. The population of the town P is modeled by the function $P(t) = 3500(0.97)^t$, where t is the number of years after 2000.

    a. By what factor did the population change between 2000 and 2001? Between 2001 and 2002? Round your answers to the nearest hundredth. Show your work. What do you notice?

    _____

    _____

    _____

    _____

    b. By what factor did the population change between 2000 and 2002? Between 2001 and 2003? Round your answers to the nearest hundredth. Show your work. What do you notice?

    _____

    _____

    _____

    _____

    _____

Getting Ready for High-Stakes Assessment   92   Algebra 1

Name _____ Date _____ Class_____

The student will recognize when one quantity changes at a constant rate per unit interval relative to another.

SELECTED RESPONSE
Select the correct answer.

1. In which of the following situations does Michael's salary change at a constant rate relative to the year?

   (A) Michael's starting salary is $9500 and increases by 4% each year.

   (B) Michael's starting salary is $9500 and increases by $500 each year.

   (C) Michael's starting salary is $9500. He receives a $500 raise after one year and a $600 raise after the second year.

   (D) Michael's starting salary is $9500. He receives a 4% raise after one year and a 5% raise after the second year.

2. Circle the phrase that makes a true statement.

   The table shows the population of two cities. The population of

City A is
City B is
both City A and City B are
neither City A nor City B is

   changing at

   a constant rate per year.

Year	City A	City B
2009	700,000	570,000
2010	697,500	580,000
2011	694,500	590,000
2012	690,500	600,000

Select all correct answers.

3. Determine which situations describe an amount of money changing at a constant rate relative to a unit change in time of the specified unit.

   (A) The value of David's car decreases by 11% each year.

   (B) Susan adds $50 to a savings account each week.

   (C) The price of a stock each week is 105% of its price from the previous week.

   (D) Monica pays $700 for car insurance the first year and pays an additional $10 per year.

   (E) The amount Ariel and Miguel pay to rent a car for $40 a day.

CONSTRUCTED RESPONSE

4. For which of these functions does the function value change at a constant rate per unit change in x? Explain.

x	$f(x)$	$g(x)$	$h(x)$
1	6	1	31
2	12	2	25
3	20	4	19
4	30	8	13
5	42	16	7

   _____

   _____

   _____

   _____

   _____

   _____

   _____

   _____

   _____

Name _____ Date _____ Class_____

5. Samantha started a new job, and is paid $10.50 an hour. Each month, Samantha earns a $0.25 per hour raise. Does Samantha's hourly pay grow at a constant rate per unit change in month? Explain.

_____

_____

_____

6. Alonzo and Katy hike 4 miles in 2 hours and then break to eat lunch. After lunch, they hike for 45 minutes and travel 1.5 miles. Not including the time spent eating lunch, do Alonzo and Katy hike at a constant rate? If not, explain why not. If so, what is the unit rate?

_____

_____

_____

7. Tim works as a salesperson for a furniture store.

His first year, he earns a base pay of $25,000 plus a 5% commission on every item he sells. His second year, he earns a base pay of $26,000 plus a 6.5% commission.

His third year, he earns a base pay of $27,040 plus an 8% commission.

Decide if each of the quantities below changes at a constant rate per unit change in year. Explain your answers.

a. Tim's base pay.

_____

_____

b. Tim's commission rate.

_____

_____

8. Companies A and B each employ 500 workers. Company A decides to increase its workforce by 10% each year. Company B decides to increase its workforce by 50 workers each year.

a. Complete the table to show each company's workforce for the first 3 years after implementing the plan to increase its workforce. Round down to the nearest person.

Year	Company A	Company B
0	500	500
1		
2		
3		

b. For each company, find the amount by which the workforce changed each year. Which company's workforce has a constant rate of growth per unit change of year? Show your work.

_____

_____

_____

_____

_____

_____

_____

_____

_____

_____

_____

c. Use your results from part b to determine that company's workforce 4 years after implementing the plan to increase its workforce.

_____

The student will recognize when one quantity changes by a constant percent rate per unit interval relative to another.

SELECTED RESPONSE

Select the correct answer.

1. In which of the following situations does Pam's hourly wage change by a constant percent per unit change in year?

   Ⓐ Pam's starting hourly wage is $14.50 per hour the first year, and it increases by $1.50 each year.

   Ⓑ Pam's starting hourly wage is $13.00. She receives a $0.50 per hour raise after one year, a $0.75 per hour raise after the second year, a $1.00 per hour raise after the third year, and so on.

   Ⓒ Pam's hourly wage is $20 per hour in the first year, $22 per hour the second year, $24.20 per hour the third year, and so on.

   Ⓓ Pam's starting hourly wage is $15.00. Her hourly wage is $15.75 after one year, $17.00 after two years, $18.75 after three years, and so on.

2. Circle the phrase that makes a true statement.

   The table shows the value, in dollars, of three cars after they are purchased.

   The value of

Car A decreases
Car B decreases
Car C decreases
Cars A and B decrease
Cars B and C decrease

   by a constant percent.

Year	Car A	Car B	Car C
0	$21,000	$18,000	$25,000
1	$18,000	$15,625	$22,500
2	$15,000	$13,250	$20,250

Select all correct answers.

3. Which of the following situations describe a quantity that increases by a constant percent that is at least 20% per unit time?

   Ⓐ There are 400 bacteria in a Petri dish the first day, 700 the second day, 1225 the third day, and so forth.

   Ⓑ The number of fish in the lake is 24 the first year, 48 in the second year, 72 in the third year, and so on.

   Ⓒ The number of visitors for a website is 4000 one month, 5200 the second month, 6760 the third month, and so on.

   Ⓓ The price for a gallon of cooking oil is $3.00 the first year, $3.30 the second year, $3.63 the third year, and so on.

   Ⓔ The population of a town is 10,000 the first year, 11,500 the second year, 13,225 the third year, and so on.

CONSTRUCTED RESPONSE

4. For which of these functions does the function value change at a constant factor per unit change in *x*? Explain.

x	*f(x)*	*g(x)*	*h(x)*
1	512	18	65
2	128	16	33
3	32	14	17
4	8	12	9
5	2	10	5

   _____

   _____

   _____

   _____

   _____

   _____

   _____

5. In one year, a population of endangered turtles laid 8000 nests. Each year, the number of nests is half as many as the number of nests in the previous year. Does the number of nests change by a constant percent per unit change in a year? Explain.

_____

_____

_____

_____

6. The table shows the mass, in grams, of the radioactive isotope carbon-11 after it starts decaying. Does the mass of the substance decay by a constant percent each minute? If so, find the decay rate. Explain and round to the nearest hundredth of a percent. If not, explain why not.

Time (minutes)	Mass (grams)
0	500
1	483.24
2	467.05
3	451.40

_____

_____

_____

_____

_____

_____

_____

_____

7. Carol inherited three antiques one year. The value, in dollars, of each antique for the first few years after she inherited the antiques is shown in the table.

Time (years)	Antique toy	Antique vase	Antique chair
0	$70.00	$25.00	$100.00
1	$77.00	$30.00	$108.00
2	$84.70	$37.50	$116.64
3	$93.17	$47.50	$125.97

Which antiques have a value that grows by a constant factor relative to time? Of those antiques, which antique increases its value at a faster rate? Explain your answers.

_____

_____

_____

8. Two competing companies redesigned their websites during the same month. The table shows the number of visits each website receives per month after the redesigns. Jeff thinks that the number of visits for both websites grows by a constant percent per month.

Month	Company A	Company B
0	120,000	150,000
1	126,000	153,000
2	132,300	157,590
3	138,915	159,166

a. Is Jeff correct about company A? Justify your answer.

_____

_____

_____

b. Is Jeff correct about company B? Justify your answer.

_____

_____

_____

The student will construct linear and exponential functions given a graph, a description, or two input-output pairs.

SELECTED RESPONSE
Select all correct answers.

1. Emile is saving money to buy a bicycle. The amount he has saved is shown in the table. Circle each function below that describes the amount A, in dollars, Emile has saved after t weeks.

Weeks	Amount
1	$30
2	$45
3	$60
4	$75
5	$90
6	$105

$A(t) = 15 + 15(t - 1)$

$A(t) = 30 + 15(t - 1)$

$A(t) = 15 + 15t$

$A(t) = 30 + 15t$

$A(t) = 30(1.5)^t$

$A(t) = 15(2)^t$

Select the correct answer.

2. Which function models the relationship between x and $f(x)$ shown in the table?

x	f(x)
2	1
4	5
6	9

Ⓐ $f(x) = \dfrac{1}{2}x$ Ⓒ $f(x) = 2x - 3$

Ⓑ $f(x) = x - 1$ Ⓓ $f(x) = 4x - 7$

3. Sasha invests $1000 that earns 8% interest compounded annually. Which function describes the value V of the investment after t years?

Ⓐ $V(t) = 1000 + 80t$

Ⓑ $V(t) = 1000(0.08)^t$

Ⓒ $V(t) = 1000(0.92)^t$

Ⓓ $V(t) = 1000(1.08)^t$

CONSTRUCTED RESPONSE

4. A $100 amount is invested in two accounts. Account 1 earns 0.25% interest compounded monthly, and account 2 earns 0.25% simple interest monthly. Write two functions that model the balances B_1 and B_2 of both accounts, in dollars, after t months.

_____

_____

5. An initial population of 1000 bacteria increases by 25% each day.

   a. Is the population growth best modeled by a linear function or an exponential function? Explain.

   _____

   _____

   b. Write a function that models the population P after t days.

   _____

6. The value of a stock over time is shown in the table. Write an exponential function that models the value V, in dollars, after t years. Show your work.

Time, in years	Value, in dollars
0	18.00
1	16.20
2	14.58
3	13.12
4	11.81
5	10.63

_____

_____

_____

7. The number of seats in each row of an auditorium can be modeled by an arithmetic sequence. The 5th row in this auditorium has 36 seats. The 12th row in this auditorium has 64 seats. Write an explicit rule for an arithmetic sequence that models the number of seats s in the nth row of the auditorium. Show your work.

_____

_____

8. The art club is creating and selling a comic book as part of a fundraiser. The graph shows the profit P earned from selling c comic books.

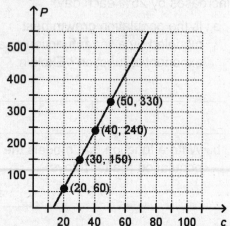

a. Use the graph to write a linear function $P(c)$ that models the profit P from selling c comic books.

_____

b. What is the real-world meaning of the slope and P-intercept of your function?

_____

c. How many comic books does the club have to sell in order to make $375? Show your work.

_____

_____

9. The neck of a guitar is divided by frets in such a way that pressing down on each fret changes the note produced when the guitar is played. The first fret of a guitar is placed 36.35 mm from the end of the guitar's neck. The second fret is placed 34.31 mm from the first fret. The distances, d, in millimeters, of the first four frets relative to the previous fret are shown in the graph below.

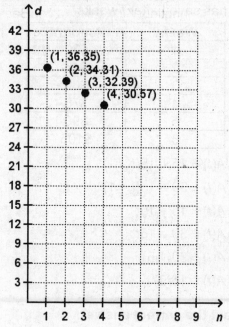

a. Consider the sequence of distances between the frets. Is the sequence arithmetic or geometric? Find a common difference or ratio to justify your answer.

_____

_____

b. Write an explicit rule for $d(n)$, the distance between fret n and the fret below it. Show your work.

_____

c. Use your rule from part b to determine the distance between the 19th and 20th frets.

_____

_____

The student will observe in tables and graphs that exponential growth will exceed linear or quadratic growth.

SELECTED RESPONSE
Select all correct answers.

1. The value V_A of stock A t months after it is purchased is modeled by the function $V_A(t) = t^2 + 1.50$. The value V_B of stock B t months after it is purchased is modeled by the function $V_B(t) = 10(1.25)^t$. Based on the model, for which t-values is the value of stock B greater than the value of stock A?

   (A) $t = 5$

   (B) $t = 6$

   (C) $t = 7$

   (D) $t = 11$

   (E) $t = 12$

Select the correct answer.

2. $f(x) = 2x^2 + 2$ and $g(x) = 2^{x+1} + 2$ are graphed on the grid below. For what x-values is $g(x) > f(x)$?

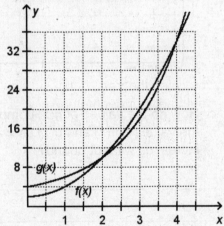

   (A) $x > 4$

   (B) $x > 2$

   (C) $0 < x < 2$ and $x > 4$

   (D) $2 < x < 4$

3. As x increases without bound, which of the following eventually has greater function values than all the others for the same values of x?

   (A) $f(x) = 3x^2$

   (B) $f(x) = 2x^3$

   (C) $f(x) = 3(2^x)$

   (D) $f(x) = 3x + 2$

4. Two websites launched at the beginning of the year. The number of visits $A(t)$ to website A is given by some exponential function, where t is the time in months after the website is launched. The number of visits $B(t)$ to website B is given by some quadratic function. The graph of each function is shown below.

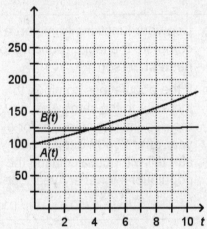

For each of the given t-values, compare $A(t)$ and $B(t)$ and put a check mark in the appropriate column of the table.

	$A(t) < B(t)$	$A(t) > B(t)$
$t = 2$		
$t = 3$		
$t = 4$		
$t = 5$		
$t > 12$		

Name _____ Date _____ Class_____

CONSTRUCTED RESPONSE

5. The population A of town A and the population B of town B t years after 2000 is described in the table.

Time, t (years)	Town A population, A(t)	Town B population, B(t)
0	1500	1500
1	1800	1725
2	2100	1984
3	2400	2281
4	2700	2624
5	3000	3017
6	3300	3470
7		
8		

a. Write functions for A(t) and B(t).

_____

_____

b. Use your functions from part a to complete the table, rounding to the nearest person.

c. If the populations continue to increase in the same way, how do the populations compare for every year after 2008? Explain how you can tell without calculating the populations for every year.

_____

_____

_____

_____

_____

_____

_____

6. Let $f(x) = x + 4$, $g(x) = x^4$, and $h(x) = 4^x$ for $x \geq 0$.

a. Graph $f(x)$ and $h(x)$.

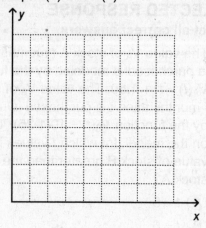

b. Graph $g(x)$ and $h(x)$.

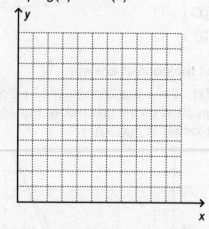

c. How do the values of $h(x)$ compare to the values of $f(x)$ and $g(x)$ as x increases without bound?

_____

_____

d. Use the graphs and your answer from part c to make a conjecture about how the values of exponential functions compare to the values of linear and polynomial functions as x increases without bound.

_____

_____

The student will interpret the parameters in a linear or exponential function in terms of a context.

SELECTED RESPONSE
Select the correct answer.

1. The function $A(d) = 0.45d + 180$ models the amount A, in dollars, that Terry's company pays him based on the round-trip distance d, in miles, that Terry travels to a job site. How much does Terry's pay increase for every mile of travel?

   (A) $0.45

   (B) $180.00

   (C) $180.45

   (D) $180.90

2. Circle the function that makes a true statement.

   Drake is considering buying one of the four popular e-readers where the e-reader's premium services is a monthly charge. The functions $A_1(t) = 5t + 350$, $A_2(t) = 10t + 250$, $A_3(t) = 499$, and $A_4(t) = 15t + 179$ model the total amount of money A, in dollars, that Drake spends after buying the e-reader and subscribing to t months of the e-reader's premium services.

   The e-reader with cost $\begin{array}{c} A_1(t) \\ A_2(t) \\ A_3(t) \\ A_4(t) \end{array}$ has the greatest monthly subscription cost.

3. Each bacterium in a petri dish splits into 2 bacteria after one day. The function $b(d) = 600 \cdot 2^d$ models the number of bacteria b in the petri dish after d days. What is the initial number of bacteria in the petri dish?

   (A) 2

   (B) 300

   (C) 600

   (D) 1200

Select all correct answers.

4. The function $a(t) = 44{,}000(1.045)^t$ models Johanna's annual earnings a, in dollars, t years after she starts her job. Which of the following statements are true about Johanna's salary?

   (A) Johanna initially earns $44,000 per year.

   (B) Johanna initially earns $45,980 per year.

   (C) Johanna's salary increases by 1.045% per year.

   (D) Johanna's salary increases by 4.5% per year.

   (E) Johanna's salary increases by 104.5% per year.

CONSTRUCTED RESPONSE

5. The function $h(t) = -1200t + 15{,}000$ models the height h, in feet, of an airplane t minutes after it starts descending in order for it to land. What is the height of the airplane when it begins to descend? Explain.

   _____

   _____

6. The function $P(r) = 256\left(\dfrac{1}{2}\right)^r$ represents the number of players P remaining after r single-elimination rounds of a tennis tournament.

   a. What is the initial number of players in the tournament? Explain.

   _____

   b. What fraction of players remaining after $r - 1$ rounds are eliminated in the rth round? Explain.

   _____

   _____

7. The function $P(r) = 1250(0.98)^t$ models the premium P, in dollars, that Steven pays for automotive insurance each year after having the insurance for t years.

   a. What is the amount that Steven pays for the first year of his insurance coverage?

   _____

   _____

   b. What is the percentage decrease of Steven's premium every year? Explain.

   _____

   _____

   _____

8. A family is traveling in a car at a constant average speed during a road trip. The function $d(t) = 65t + 715$ models the distance d, in miles, the family is from their house t hours after starting to drive on the second day of the road trip.

   a. At what average speed is the family's car traveling? Explain.

   _____

   _____

   _____

   b. What is the distance between the family's house and the point where they started driving on the second day? Explain.

   _____

   _____

   _____

   _____

9. A census from the government determines the official population of jurisdictions. The census is taken once every decade. The function $A(c) = 50,600(1.08)^c$ models the official value for the population of city A, where c is the number of censuses taken since the first census. Similarly, $B(c) = 75,850(1.069)^c$ models the official value for the population of city B.

   a. Which city had a larger population in the first census? Explain.

   _____

   _____

   _____

   b. Which city's official value for its population is growing at a faster rate between the censuses? Explain.

   _____

   _____

   _____

   _____

The student will represent data with plots on the real number line (dot plots, histograms, and box plots).

SELECTED RESPONSE

Select the correct answer.

1. The data sets below show the numbers of cookies purchased by students at a bake sale. Which of the data sets is represented by the dot plot?

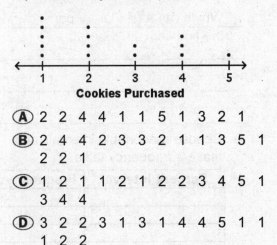

Cookies Purchased

Ⓐ 2 2 4 4 1 1 5 1 3 2 1

Ⓑ 2 4 4 2 3 3 2 1 1 3 5 1
2 2 1

Ⓒ 1 2 1 1 2 1 2 2 3 4 5 1
3 4 4

Ⓓ 3 2 2 3 1 3 1 4 4 5 1 1
1 2 2

2. The data below are the percent change in population of 20 states between 1950 and 1960. Which of the following set of intervals should be used to make a histogram of the data?

3.7   5.3   6.8   7   8.1   10.2   13.3   13.7
14.7   15.5   18.3   21.8   21.9   21.9
24.1   25.5   31.1   31.5   39.4   39.9

Ⓐ 5.0% to 9.9%, 10.0% to 19.9%, 20.0% to 29.9%, and 30.0% to 34.9%

Ⓑ 0.0% to 9.9%, 10.0% to 19.9%, 20.0% to 29.9%, and 30.0% to 39.9%

Ⓒ 0.0% to 9.9%, 10.0% to 14.9%, 15.0% to 19.9%, 20.0% to 24.9%, 25.0% to 29.9%, and 30.0% to 39.9%

Ⓓ 0.0% to 9.9%, 10.0% to 29.9%, and 30% to 39.9%

Select all correct answers.

3. The data below are the distances (in megaparsecs) from Earth of several nebulae outside the Milky Way galaxy.

0.032	0.214	0.263	0.450
0.500	0.800	0.900	1.000
1.100	1.400	1.700	2.000

Circle each number of megaparsecs below (rounded to three decimal places) that is used to make a box plot of the data.

0.032   0.357   0.377   0.850

0.863   1.250   1.350   2.000

CONSTRUCTED RESPONSE

4. The data below are the number of beds in a sample of 15 nursing homes in New Mexico in 1988.

44   59   59   60   62   65   80   80   90
96   100   110   116   120   135

a. Find the minimum and maximum of the data.

_____

b. Find the first, second, and third quartiles.

_____

c. Make a box plot of the data.

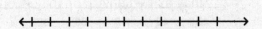

5. The data below are the average annual starting salaries (in thousands of dollars) of 20 randomly selected college graduates. Make a dot plot of the data values.

42 37 40 37 45 39 43 47 36
34 40 43 42 40 37 44 36 46
39 35

6. For the following data, create a dot plot and a box plot.

1 7 4 15 10 3 17 6 14 14 3
6 9 7 11

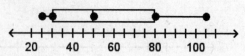

7. Billy incorrectly made a box plot for the following data. His work is shown below. Identify and correct his errors.

The following data are the amounts of potassium, in grams, per serving in randomly selected breakfast cereals.

25 25 30 30 35 35 40 45 50
55 60 60 60 70 85 90 95 95
105

Billy's box plot:

8. The following data values are the percents of the vote that the Democratic candidate won in 20 randomly selected states in the 1984 presidential election.

37.5 33.9 43.1 48.1 27.9 48.7
42.3 39.0 20.9 45.6 26.4 28.7
30.1 35.5 38.2 47.7 41.8 44.0
47.5 48.6

a. Order the data.

_____

_____

_____

_____

b. Choose reasonable intervals and make a frequency table.

Percent Interval	Frequency

c. Create a histogram of the data.

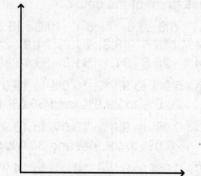

The student will use statistics appropriate to the shape of the distribution to compare center and spread of data sets.

SELECTED RESPONSE
Select the correct answer.

1. What is the best measure of center to use to compare the two data sets?
   Grams of sugar per serving in cereal brand A:

   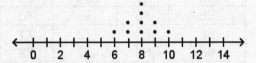

   Grams of sugar per serving in cereal brand B:

   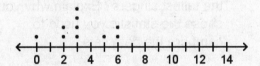

   Ⓐ Median
   Ⓑ Either the mean or the median
   Ⓒ Interquartile range
   Ⓓ Either the standard deviation or the interquartile range

2. What is the best measure of center to use to compare the two data sets?
   Data Set A:

   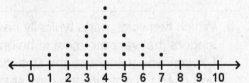

   Data Set B:

   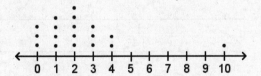

   Ⓐ Median
   Ⓑ Either the mean or the median
   Ⓒ Interquartile range
   Ⓓ Either the standard deviation or the interquartile range

3. What is the best measure of spread to use to compare the two data sets?
   Income of ten recent graduates from college A (in thousands of dollars per year):

   0 35 38 39 45 47 50 51 52 52

   Income of ten recent graduates from college B (in thousands of dollars per year):

   29 35 36 37 38 39 41 42 46 400

   Ⓐ Median
   Ⓑ Either the mean or the median
   Ⓒ Interquartile range
   Ⓓ Either the standard deviation or the interquartile range

Select all correct answers.

4. Set A below is skewed left, set B is roughly symmetric, and set C is skewed right.

Set A	Set B	Set C
23	35	40
42	38	42
43	42	44
48	45	45
55	49	45
56	52	47
57	57	49
59	61	70

   Circle each value below that should be used to compare the spread of the data sets.

   5.0   8.5   8.8   13.5
   14.0   14.5   46.9   47.8

CONSTRUCTED RESPONSE

5. The annual salaries (in thousands of dollars) of 15 randomly selected employees at two small companies are given. Indicate the shape of the data distributions. Then, compare the center and spread of the data and justify your method of doing so.

   Company 1:

   22 36 37 37 37 39 39 42 42
   45 45 46 46 150 200

   Company 2:

   21 37 38 38 38 39 42 45 45
   46 46 47 48 62 250

   _____

   _____

   _____

   _____

   _____

   _____

   _____

   _____

   _____

   _____

   _____

   _____

   _____

   _____

6. The heights, in inches, of randomly selected members of a choral company are given according to their voice part.

Soprano (in.)	Alto (in.)	Tenor (in.)	Bass (in.)
60	60	64	66
62	61	66	68
62	62	66	68
64	63	67	69
65	64	68	70
65	65	70	70
66	66	72	71
66	69	73	72
67	70	74	73
68	72	76	75

   a. Which two voice parts typically have the tallest singers? Explain why you chose the statistic you used to compare the data sets.

   _____

   _____

   _____

   _____

   _____

   _____

   b. Which two voice parts typically have singers that vary the most in height? Explain why you chose the statistic you used to compare the data sets.

   _____

   _____

   _____

   _____

   _____

   _____

Name _____ Date _____ Class _____

The student will interpret differences in shape, center, and spread in data sets, including effects of extreme data points.

SELECTED RESPONSE
Select all correct answers.

1. If the extreme values are removed from this data set, which of the following statistics change by more than 1?

10	40	41	41	42
42	43	43	43	44
45	45	45	46	65

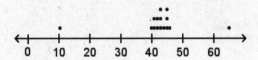

    0   10   20   30   40   50   60

Ⓐ Mean

Ⓑ Standard deviation

Ⓒ Median

Ⓓ Interquartile range

Ⓔ Range

Select the correct answer.

2. The data set below shows 15 students' scores on a test. Describe the shape of the data distribution if the student who scored 100 is not included in the data set.

70	72	73	74	74
75	75	75	75	76
77	77	78	80	100

Ⓐ The data distribution is skewed right.

Ⓑ The data distribution is symmetric.

Ⓒ The data distribution is skewed left.

Ⓓ It is impossible to determine the shape of the data distribution.

3. The ages of ten employees at a small company are shown below.

30, 32, 35, 35, 38, 38, 38, 40, 40, 45

If the data set were expanded to include a new employee who is 20 years old, how would the mean of the data set change?

Ⓐ The mean decreases by 2 years.

Ⓑ The mean decreases by about 1.6 years.

Ⓒ The mean increases by about 1.6 years.

Ⓓ The mean does not change.

4. The data set gives the batting averages of 12 professional baseball players last season. Indicate by putting a check mark in the appropriate column of the table how each of the statistics changes if the value 0.360 is removed from the data set.

    0.360   0.325   0.325   0.319   0.305   0.296

    0.296   0.291   0.285   0.279   0.279   0.277

	Decreases	No change	Increases
Mean			
Median			
Standard deviation			
Interquartile range			
Range			

Name _____   Date _____   Class _____

CONSTRUCTED RESPONSE

5. The values of several homes sold by a realtor are listed below.

| $150,000 | $175,000 | $175,000 | $200,000 | $200,000 |
| $200,000 | $225,000 | $250,000 | $250,000 | $400,000 |

 a. Create a line plot for the data, where the points represent the values in thousands of dollars. Describe the shape of the data.

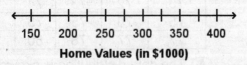

Home Values (in $1000)

 b. What value(s) in the data set are outliers? Explain.

 _____

 _____

 c. If the outlier(s) from part b are removed, how do the median and interquartile range change? How does the shape of the data change?

 _____

 _____

6. The table shows Amanda's scores on her last 15 quizzes.

70	72	75	76	76
77	78	80	80	82
83	84	87	90	90

 Suppose on her next quiz, Amanda scores a 96.

 a. How does the shape of the data distribution change if 96 is included?

 _____

 _____

 b. How does the mean of the data set change if 96 is included? the median?

 _____

 _____

 _____

 c. How does the standard deviation change if 96 is included? the interquartile range? Round your answers to the nearest tenth.

 _____

 _____

 _____

The student will use two-way frequency tables, interpret relative frequencies, and find possible trends in data.

SELECTED RESPONSE
Select the correct answer.

1. Carly surveyed some of her fellow students to determine whether they are more afraid of spiders or snakes, are equally afraid of both, or are afraid of neither. She organized the data into the two-way relative frequency table below. What is the joint relative frequency of the students surveyed who are boys and are equally afraid of both snakes and spiders?

	Spiders	Snakes	Both	Neither	Total
Boys	0.23	0.17	0.06	0.04	0.49
Girls	0.21	0.19	0.09	0.02	0.51
Total	0.43	0.36	0.15	0.06	1

(Note: Rounding may cause the totals to be off by 0.01.)

- (A) 0.06
- (B) 0.09
- (C) 0.15
- (D) 0.40

Select all correct answers.

2. Which of the following statements are supported by the survey data in the two-way frequency table?

	Right-handed	Left-handed	Total
Males	82	23	105
Females	79	16	95
Total	161	39	200

- (A) The joint relative frequency that a person surveyed is female and left-handed is about 0.168, or 16.8%.
- (B) The conditional relative frequency that a person surveyed is female, given that the person is right-handed, is about 0.4907, or 49.07%.
- (C) The joint relative frequency that a person surveyed is male and is right-handed is about 0.41, or 41%.
- (D) The conditional relative frequency that a person surveyed is right-handed, given that the person is male, is about 0.5093, or 50.93%.
- (E) The marginal relative frequency that a person surveyed is left-handed is about 0.195, or 19.5%.

Name _____ Date _____ Class_____

Match each situation and its frequency.

A magazine conducts a survey of a high school graduating class to ask whether the students plan to attend a four-year college, attend a two-year college, enter the military, or get a job. The results are given in the two-way frequency table.

	Women	Men	Total
Four-Year College	63	75	138
Two-Year College	12	18	30
Military	8	10	18
Job	15	10	25
Total	98	113	211

Choose from the values given below to match the situation with its value, rounded to two decimal places as necessary.

3. The joint relative frequency of students surveyed who are men and plan to attend a four-year college

4. The marginal relative frequency of students surveyed who plan to enter the military

5. The conditional relative frequency that a student plans to get a job, given that the student is a woman

6. The conditional relative frequency that a student is a woman, given that the student plans to attend a two-year college

0.06
0.07
0.09
0.15
0.36
0.65

CONSTRUCTED RESPONSE

7. The manager of a factory tested 50 items produced during each of the three work shifts. The data are summarized in the two-way frequency table below.

	1st shift	2nd shift	3rd shift	Total
Not defective	48	49	41	138
Defective	2	1	9	12
Total	50	50	50	150

   a. What is the conditional relative frequency that a tested item is defective, given that it was produced during the first shift? during the second shift? during the third shift?

   _____

   _____

   _____

   b. Does one shift seem more likely to produce a defective product than the other two shifts? Explain using the results from part a.

   _____

   _____

   _____

   _____

   _____

Name _____ Date _____ Class_____

The student will fit a function to data and use functions fitted to data to solve problems in the context of the data.

SELECTED RESPONSE
Select the correct answer.

1. Circle the equation that makes a true statement.

   The data for the distance d, in miles, remaining for a train to travel to its destination t hours after it departs a station are shown in the scatter plot.

   The function

   | $d(t) = 50t + 300$ |
   | $d(t) = 50t$ |
   | $d(t) = -50t + 300$ |
   | $d(t) = -50t$ |

   best fits the data.

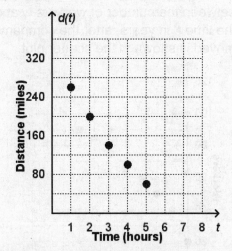

2. Darnell is tracking the number of touchdowns t and the number of points p his favorite football team scores each game this season. He made a scatter plot to display the data. Which of the following functions for the relationship between the number of points scored per game and the number of touchdowns scored per game could be the line of best fit passing through the points (1, 10), (3, 24), and (5, 38) on the scatter plot?

   Ⓐ $p(t) = 7$

   Ⓑ $p(t) = 7t + 3$

   Ⓒ $p(t) = -7t + 3$

   Ⓓ $p(t) = 7t - 3$

Select all correct answers.

3. Emile collects data about the amount of oil A, in gallons, used to heat his house per month for 5 months and the average monthly temperature t, in degrees Fahrenheit, for those months. The scatter plot shows the data. The function $A(t) = -1.4t + 96$ best fits these data. Use $A(t)$ to determine which of the following statements are true.

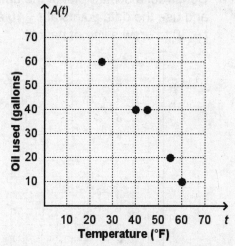

   Ⓐ Emile would use about 82 gallons of oil to heat his house for a month with average temperature 10 °F.

   Ⓑ Emile would use about 85 gallons of oil to heat his house for a month with average temperature 15 °F.

   Ⓒ Emile would use 0 gallons of oil to heat his house for a month with average temperature 70 °F.

   Ⓓ Emile would use about 5 gallons of oil to heat his house for a month with average temperature 55 °F.

   Ⓔ Emile would use 96 gallons of oil to heat his house for a month with average temperature 0 °F.

Name _____ Date _____ Class_____

CONSTRUCTED RESPONSE

4. The data for the height h, in meters, a hot air balloon is above the ground in terms of time t, in minutes, after it starts descending are shown in the table.

Time, t (minutes)	Height, h (meters)
10	1100
15	900
20	800
25	700
30	500

a. Construct a scatter plot of the data and use the data points at $t = 10$ and $t = 30$ to draw a line of best fit.

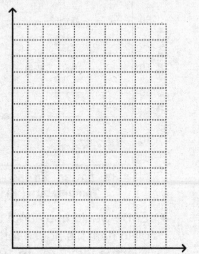

b. Use the results from part a to write a linear function that represents the line of best fit. Show your work.

_____

_____

_____

_____

_____

_____

c. Use the linear function from part b to predict the height of the hot air balloon when it started to descend. Explain.

_____

_____

d. Use the linear function from part b to predict how long, to the nearest minute, it takes for the hot air balloon to descend to the ground. Explain.

_____

_____

5. A company moved to a new office building 8 years ago. The relationship between the number of workers w and the time t, in years, after the company moved is shown in the scatter plot.

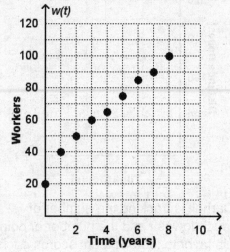

Suppose a linear function that fits the data is $w(t) = \dfrac{25}{3}t + \dfrac{95}{3}$. Using that result and the point corresponding to $t = 8$, predict the number of new workers the company will have two years from now. Explain.

_____

_____

_____

Name _____ Date _____ Class_____

The student will informally assess the fit of a function by plotting and analyzing residuals.

SELECTED RESPONSE

Select all correct answers.

1. The table shows the median weight, in pounds, of babies born at a particular hospital for the first 6 months after they are born. The line $y = 1.7x + 8.1$ is fit to the data in the table, resulting in the residual plot below.

Age (months)	Median weight (pounds)
0	7.4
1	9.9
2	12.3
3	13.1
4	15.4
5	16.9
6	17.5

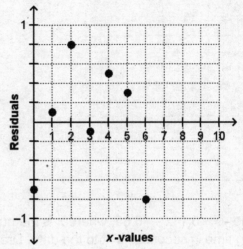

Circle each statement that is true.

The residuals do not appear to follow a pattern.

The residuals are mostly below the x-axis.

The residuals are relatively small compared to the data values.

The residuals are relatively large compared to the data values.

The line is a good fit to the data.

Select the correct answer.

2. The plot shows the residuals when a line is fit to a set of data. Based on the residual plot, which statement *best* describes how well the line fits the data?

Ⓐ The line is a good fit because the residuals are all close to the x-axis and are randomly distributed about the x-axis.

Ⓑ The line is not a good fit because the residuals are not all close to the x-axis.

Ⓒ The line is not a good fit because the residuals are not randomly distributed about the x-axis

Ⓓ The line is not a good fit because the residuals are not all close to the x-axis and are not randomly distributed about the x-axis.

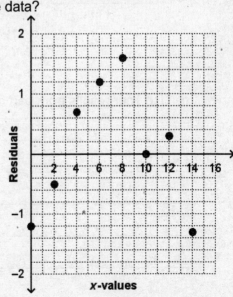

CONSTRUCTED RESPONSE

3. The table shows the time, in seconds, of the men's gold-medal-winning 400 m runner at the Olympics from 1948 to 1968.

Year	1948	1952	1956	1960	1964	1968
Time (sec)	46.30	46.09	46.85	45.07	45.15	43.86

a. Draw a scatter plot of the data.

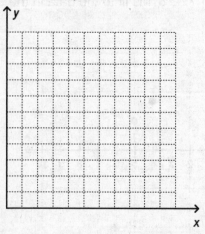

b. The line $y = -0.14x + 46.65$, where x is the number of years after 1948 and y is the winning time in seconds, is fit to the data. Draw the line on the scatter plot.

c. Complete the table with the values predicted by the function in part b, and then plot the residuals on the graph below.

Year	Actual time (sec)	Predicted time (sec)	Residual (sec)
1948	46.30		
1952	46.09		
1956	46.85		
1960	45.07		
1964	45.15		
1968	43.86		

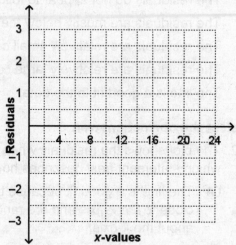

d. Use your results from part c to describe the fit of the line.

_____

_____

_____

_____

_____

Name _____ Date _____ Class _____

The student will fit a linear function for a scatter plot that suggests a linear association.

SELECTED RESPONSE
Select the correct answer.

1. Circle the value that makes a true statement.

   The scatter plot shown suggests the association between the values of x with the values of y is linear. The y-intercept of the linear function that represents the line of best fit is $\boxed{\begin{matrix} -1.96 \\ 11.15 \\ 11.41 \\ 22.36 \end{matrix}}$, rounded to two decimal places.

   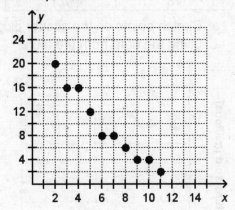

2. The scatter plot shows the relationship between the time t, in years after 1900, and the life expectancy L, in years, at birth for a certain country. Do the data on the scatter plot suggest a linear association? If so, what is a function that represents the line of best fit?

   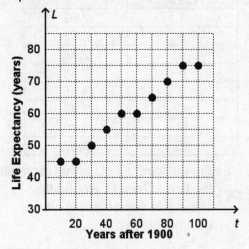

   (A) Yes; $L(t) = 39.67t + 0.37$

   (B) Yes; $L(t) = -0.24t + 74.33$

   (C) Yes; $L(t) = 0.37t + 39.67$

   (D) No; the data on the scatter plot do not suggest a linear association.

Select all correct answers.

3. The relationship between the amount of data downloaded d, in megabytes, and the time t, in seconds, after the download started is shown. The data points on the scatter plot suggest a linear association. Which of the following statements are true?

   (A) The data points on the scatter plot suggest a negative correlation.

   (B) The data points on the scatter plot suggest a positive correlation.

   (C) For every second that passes, about 1 additional megabyte is downloaded.

   (D) For every second that passes, about 0.5 additional megabyte is downloaded.

   (E) The function that represents the line of best fit is approximately $d(t) = 0.51t - 1.04$.

   (F) The function that represents the line of best fit is approximately $d(t) = 1.04t + 0.51$.

   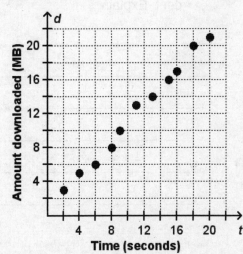

CONSTRUCTED RESPONSE

4. The table shows the relationship between the average price for a gallon of milk p, in dollars, in terms of time t, in years after 1995. When the data is plotted on a scatter plot, the data suggest a linear association.

Time, t (years after 1995)	Price, p (dollars)
1	2.62
3	2.70
5	2.78
6	2.88
9	3.15
12	3.40
14	3.30
16	3.57

a. Find a linear function that represents the line of best fit. Round the slope and p-intercept to two decimal places.

_____

_____

_____

_____

b. Use the results from part a to estimate the average price for a gallon of milk in 2006 to the nearest cent. Explain.

_____

_____

_____

_____

_____

_____

5. A bottled water company is examining the sales of its product. The executives are analyzing the number of bottles sold per year b, in millions, as a function of time t, in years since 1990. The data are shown in the table.

Time, t (years)	Bottles sold, b (millions)
1	1.6
3	2.3
5	3.1
6	3.5
8	4.2
9	4.4
11	5.1
14	5.9
16	6.4
18	7.1

a. Sketch points on the scatter plot using the data from the table.

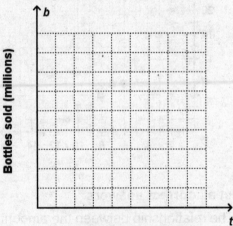

Time (years after 1990)

b. The function $b(t) = 0.32t + 1.47$ represents the line of best fit for the data. About how many more bottles were sold in 2007 than in 1992? Explain.

_____

_____

_____

_____

The student will interpret the slope and the intercept of a linear model in the context of the data.

SELECTED RESPONSE
Select the correct answer.

1. The linear equation
   $c = 0.1998s + 76.4520$ models the
   number of calories c in a beef hot dog
   as a function of the amount of sodium s,
   in milligrams, in the hot dog. What is
   the slope, and what does it mean in
   this context?

   (A) The slope is 0.1998. The number of
   calories is increased by 0.1998 for
   each 1 milligram increase in sodium.

   (B) The slope is 0.1998. The amount of
   sodium, in milligrams, is increased by
   0.1699 for each increase of 1 calorie.

   (C) The slope is 76.4520. This is the
   number of calories in a beef hot dog
   with no sodium.

   (D) The slope is 76.4520. This is the
   amount of sodium, in milligrams, in a
   beef hot dog with no calories.

2. The linear equation $c = 6.5n + 1500$
   models cost c, in dollars, to produce
   n toys at a toy factory. What is the
   c-intercept, and what does it mean in this
   context?

   (A) The c-intercept is 6.5. The cost
   increases by \$6.50 for each toy
   produced.

   (B) The c-intercept is 6.5. The number of
   toys produced increases by about 6.5
   for each \$1 increase in cost.

   (C) The c-intercept is 1500. It costs
   \$1500 to run the factory if no toys are
   produced.

   (D) The c-intercept is 1500. The factory
   can produce 1500 toys at no cost.

3. The linear equation $p = 2376t + 73{,}219$ estimates the number of college seniors p who
   graduated with a bachelor's degree in psychology t years after 2000. The linear equation
   $b = 2{,}376t + 56{,}545$ models the number of college seniors b who graduated with a
   bachelor's degree in biology t years after 2000. Indicate by putting a check mark in the
   appropriate column of the table whether each statement is true or false according to the
   given models.

	True	False
The number of psychology degrees increases by about 73,219 each year.		
The number of biology degrees increases by about 2376 each year.		
About 73,000 students graduated with degrees in psychology in 2000.		
About 57 students graduated with degrees in biology in 2000.		
In 2000, more students graduated with psychology degrees than biology degrees.		

CONSTRUCTED RESPONSE

4. The function $d(t) = 2.05t + 1.27$ models the depth of the water d, in centimeters, of a filling bathtub at time t, in minutes. What does the slope of the function represent in the context of the problem? What does the d-intercept represent in the context of the problem? Include any units in your answers.

_____

_____

_____

_____

5. The function $c(r) = 2r + 12.5$ represents the cost c, in dollars, of riding r rides at a carnival.

   a. How much does it cost to get into the carnival? Explain.

   _____

   _____

   _____

   _____

   b. How much does each ride cost? Explain.

   _____

   _____

   _____

   _____

6. The table below shows the height h, in meters, of a tree that is t years old.

Age (in years)	Height (in meters)
1	0.7
2	1.3
3	1.8
4	2.5
5	3.1
6	3.8
7	4.2
8	4.9
9	5.5
10	6.2

   a. Make a scatter plot of the data from the table.

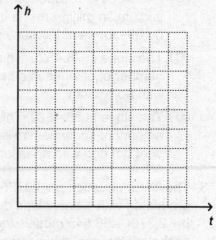

   b. Find a line of best fit.

   _____

   _____

   c. Identify and interpret the slope of the line from part b.

   _____

   _____

   d. Identify and interpret the h-intercept of the line from part b.

   _____

   _____

Name _____ Date _____ Class _____

The student will compute (using technology) and interpret the correlation coefficient of a linear fit.

SELECTED RESPONSE

Select all correct answers.

1. Which of the following correlation coefficients indicate a strong linear correlation?

   (A) −0.872691

   (B) −0.658799

   (C) −0.125866

   (D) 0.568962

   (E) 0.798264

   (F) 0.989862

Select the correct answer.

2. What is the correlation coefficient of linear fit for the following data set? Use technology to find the correlation coefficient. Assume *x* is the independent variable.

x	y
1.4	4.7
2.3	5.0
4.5	7.4
5.8	8.6
3.2	6.7
1.9	4.2
8.7	11.4
5.5	8.0
6.7	10.4

   (A) −0.982478

   (B) −0.328699

   (C) 0.328699

   (D) 0.982478

3. Circle the phrase that makes a true statement.

   The linear correlation in the following data, using *x* as the dependent variable,

   is a [strong negative / weak negative / weak positive / strong positive] correlation.

x	y
1.2	5.3
3.2	6.7
3.3	3.3
4.5	4.3
6.1	5.5
6.3	2.1
7.1	0.5
9.6	0.75
9	4.1

   (Use technology if necessary.)

CONSTRUCTED RESPONSE

4. Consider the following scatter plot. Use technology to find the line of best fit, using *x* as the independent variable and *y* as the dependent variable. What happens to *y* as *x* increases? Find the correlation coefficient. How strong a fit is the line? Explain.

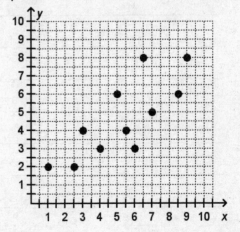

_____

_____

_____

5. The table lists the latitude of several cities in the Northern Hemisphere along with their average annual temperatures.

City	Latitude	Average Annual Temp.
Bangkok, Thailand	13.7°N	82.6 °F
Cairo, Egypt	30.1°N	71.4 °F
London, England	51.5°N	51.8 °F
Moscow, Russia	55.8°N	39.4 °F
New Delhi, India	28.6°N	77.0 °F
Tokyo, Japan	35.7°N	58.1 °F
Vancouver, Canada	49.2°N	49.6 °F

a. Use technology to find the correlation coefficient of a linear fit using latitude as the independent variable and average annual temperature as the dependent variable.

_____

b. Describe the correlation. Explain how you arrived at your answer.

_____
_____
_____
_____
_____
_____
_____
_____
_____
_____

6. The table shows the annual expenditures on entertainment and reading per person over 10 years. Between entertainment and reading, which is more strongly correlated with the passage of time? Describe each correlation as part of your answer.

Year	Entertainment	Reading
2000	$1863	$146
2001	$1953	$141
2002	$2079	$139
2003	$2060	$127
2004	$2218	$130
2005	$2388	$126
2006	$2376	$117
2007	$2698	$118
2008	$2835	$116
2009	$2693	$110

_____
_____
_____
_____
_____
_____
_____
_____
_____
_____
_____
_____
_____
_____
_____
_____
_____

The student will distinguish between correlation and causation.

SELECTED RESPONSE
Select the correct answer.

1. Susan measures her son Jeremy's height at various ages. The results are shown below. Which of the following is a statement of causation?

Age (years)	Height (inches)
8	44
9	48
10	52
11	55
12	58
13	62

Ⓐ When Jeremy was 13 years old, he was 62 inches tall.

Ⓑ There appears to be a relationship between Jeremy's age and height.

Ⓒ As Jeremy's age increases, his height also increases.

Ⓓ Jeremy's age affects his height.

Select all correct answers.

2. Jewelers consider weight, cut grade, color, and clarity when pricing diamonds. In researching jewelry prices, Yvonne makes the following statements based on her observations. Which of the statements are statements of causation?

Ⓐ Heavier diamonds tend to be sold at higher prices.

Ⓑ A particular diamond costs $264.

Ⓒ Higher clarity drives up the price of a diamond.

Ⓓ There appears to be a relationship between color and price.

Ⓔ A darker color decreases a diamond's clarity.

Ⓕ Diamonds with lower cut grades seem to sell at lower prices.

3. Indicate by putting a check mark in the appropriate column of the table whether each statement is a statement of correlation, a statement of causation, or neither.

	Correlation	Causation	Neither
Taller people tend to have bigger hands.			
Being tall makes your hands bigger.			
Shorter people tend to have smaller hands.			
Being short makes your hands smaller.			
I'm 6'8" and I have bigger hands than anyone else in my family.			

Name _____ Date _____ Class_____

CONSTRUCTED RESPONSE

4. The table below shows the approximate diameters (in miles) and number of moons for each of the eight planets in our solar system. Calculate the correlation coefficient, r, of the data to three decimal places. What kind of correlation, if any, exists between diameter and number of moons? Does a planet's diameter influence the number of moons it has? Explain.

Planet	Diameter (miles)	Moons
Mercury	3032	0
Venus	7521	0
Earth	7926	1
Mars	4222	2
Jupiter	88,846	62
Saturn	74,898	33
Uranus	31,763	27
Neptune	30,778	13

_____

_____

_____

_____

_____

_____

_____

_____

_____

_____

_____

5. The table below lists the departure delay times (in minutes) and arrival delay times (in minutes) for 10 flights. (A negative delay time means a flight departed/arrived ahead of schedule.)

Departure Delay Times (minutes)	Arrival Delay Times (minutes)
−10	−7
−5	−6
0	−1
0	1
5	3
8	10
10	7
10	12
15	15
20	23

a. Is there a correlation between departure delay times and arrival delay times? Explain.

_____

_____

_____

b. Are departure delay times responsible for all arrival delay times? Explain.

_____

_____

_____

c. Are arrival delay times responsible for all departure delay times? Explain.

_____

_____

_____

_____